POWER
OF POTENTIAL

Maximize God's Principles to Fulfill Your Dreams

MAJORING IN MEN®
The Curriculum for Men

Edwin Louis Cole

**WHITAKER
HOUSE**

Unless otherwise indicated, all Scripture quotations are taken from the King James Version of the Holy Bible. Scripture quotations marked (AMP) are taken from the *Amplified® Bible*, © 1954, 1958, 1962, 1964, 1965, 1987 by The Lockman Foundation. Used by permission. (www. Lockman.org). Scripture quotations marked (TLB) are taken from *The Living Bible*, © 1971. Used by permission of Tyndale House Publishers, Inc., Wheaton, Illinois 60189. All rights reserved.

POWER OF POTENTIAL WORKBOOK:
Maximize God's Principles to Fulfill Your Dreams

Christian Men's Network
P.O. Box 3
Grapevine, TX 76099
(817) 437-4888
www.ChristianMensNetwork.com

Facebook.com/EdwinLouisCole

ISBN: 979-8-88769-150-3
Printed in the United States of America
© 2014 Edwin and Nancy Cole Legacy LLC

Published by:
Whitaker House
1030 Hunt Valley Circle
New Kensington, PA 15068

Majoring in Men® and Resolute Books™ are registered trademarks of Edwin and Nancy Cole Legacy LLC.

This book has been printed digitally and produced in a standard specification in order to ensure its continuing availability.

TABLE OF CONTENTS

Lesson 1

To Dream the Impossible Dream

Lesson 1

To Dream the Impossible Dream

A.   Dreams are the substance of every great achievement.

Which of the following were created by men who dreamed? *(circle all that apply)* *(pages 9-10)*

   1.   The Golden Gate Bridge in San Francisco

   2.   New York City

   3.   Modern Romania

   4.   The Declaration of Independence

B.   Truth is synonymous with: *(circle one)* *(page 11)*

reality   trust   self-confidence

   1.   Everything God does, He does according to a _____ based upon a _____

   _____ of His Kingdom. *(page 11)*

For Further Study

Truth is not an option in life – Zechariah 8:16. Truth is the bedrock of integrity. Your integrity is the cornerstone of your character – Psalm 24:4, 5.

Everything God does is according to a pattern, based on a principle – *"See, saith he, that thou make all things according to the pattern shown to thee in the mount"* Hebrews 8:5; *"May God's mercy and peace be upon all of you who live by this principle and upon those everywhere who are really God's own"* Galatians 6:16 TLB; Exodus 25:8, 9; 1 Chronicles 28:11.

All principles of human society are basically Kingdom principles – Romans 11:36; 1 Corinthians 8:6; Colossians 1:16-17.

God promises to give us the desires of our hearts – Psalms 21:2; 145:19; Proverbs 10:24.

2. What is a key that unlocks Heaven to us? *(page 11)*

    _____

3. The more you base your life on personality, the better off you'll be. *(page 11)*

    ____ True   ____ False

C. Look up and read out loud Hebrews 11:1 and Hebrews 12:1-3.

    1. God will finish what He _____, but He is not obligated to _____

        what He has not _____. *(page 12)*

    2. Without a dream, some are without _____. Without _____, life is hopeless. *(page 13)*

D. In your experience, how do men you know act and who do they blame when they have unfulfilled

    dreams? *(page 14)*

    _____

For Further Study

God authors those desires – *"Delight thyself also in the Lord; and he shall give thee the desires of thine heart"* Psalm 37:4.

God implements those desires as we submit to His Lordship – *"Commit thy way unto the Lord; trust also in him; and he shall bring it to pass"* Psalm 37:5.

The more we base our lives on principles, the straighter our course will be – Proverbs 4:11-12.

A shattered dream is devastating to an individual – Proverbs 13:12.

Dreams that are nothing more than fantasies cannot stand the test of reality – *"For in the multitude of dreams and many words there are also divers vanities: but fear thou God"* Ecclesiastes 5:7.

What God authors, He will finish – Philippians 1:6; *"Looking unto Jesus the author and finisher of our faith"* Hebrews 12:2.

E.   Read about Joseph in Genesis 37.

F.   Joseph's dream was God's revelation of _____. *(page 14)*

    1.   There is a _____ for leadership. Joseph's was spending thirteen years

        in _____ with temptation and accusation. *(page 15)*

    2.   All testing is based on _____. Your ability to resist the devil is proportionate to

        your _____ to God. *(page 15)*

    3.   Look up James 4:7 and restate **in your own words.**

        _____

        _____

G.   Write out Proverbs 8:17. _____

    _____

    Submitting to God in the _____ will give men the _____ to resist

    the devil in the _____. *(page 15)*

For Further Study

What God promises, He will fulfill – *"God is not a man, that he should lie; neither the son of man, that he should repent: hath he said, and shall he not do it? or hath he spoken, and shall he not make it good?"* Numbers 23:19.
What is committed to God, He will keep – 2 Timothy 1:12; Titus 1:2; *"Now unto him that is able to keep you from falling, and to present you faultless before the presence of his glory with exceeding joy"* Jude 24.
Dreams are one of the ways God speaks to us – *"I the Lord will ... speak unto him in a dream"* Numbers 12:6.
Joseph's dream was a revelation of leadership – Genesis 37:7-9.
God prepares leaders through testing – Hebrews 2:10.
There is a price to pay in leadership – Philippians 2:5-8.

H. Preparation is the _____ for success. *(page 15)*

1. Some men don't want to pay the price of _____ to prepare. *(page 16)*

2. Name some Bible men who learned to handle themselves. *(page 16)*

a. _____   c. _____

b. _____   d. _____

Circle the ones who achieved their dreams or purpose in life.

3. Read Proverbs 16:32 and restate it **in your own words.** _____

_____

I. Joseph identified with God. His brothers identified with: *(page 16)* _____

_____

1. Flattery is disguised _____. *(page 17)*

2. _____ will always outlast persecution. *(page 18)*

For Further Study

Ruling the spirit is a requirement of successful leadership – Proverbs 16:32; 25:28.

Testing is always based on resistance – James 1:12.

Your ability to resist the devil is proportionate to your submission to the Lord – *"Submit yourselves therefore to God. Resist the devil, and he will flee from you"* James 4:7.

Without submitting to the Lord in the morning, there is no ability to resist the devil in the afternoon – Psalms 5; 63:1; Proverbs 8:17.

Joseph identified with the dream God gave him – Genesis 37:6.

His brothers identified with the flesh, their personal desires – Genesis 37:8, 11, 23-24.

They identified Joseph with their own selfish spirits and attributed to him the motives of their own hearts – Genesis 50:15; *"Unto the pure all things are pure: but unto them that are defiled and unbelieving is nothing pure; but even their mind and conscience is defiled"* Titus 1:15.

J. You are never too young, too old, too poor or too rich for God to make your dream a reality. *(page 18)* Write out Romans 2:11.

_____

_____

K. God-given dreams in God-favored men make a _____ world. *(page 18)*

Practical:

1. Name three things you identify yourself with. _____

_____

Circle the ones that God authored. What ones do you need to change? _____

_____

2. From this chapter, name three things you need to do or need to have to achieve your dreams.

_____

_____

For Further Study

Perseverance will always outlast persecution – James 1:4; *"But the God of all grace, who hath called us unto his eternal glory by Christ Jesus, after that ye have suffered a while, make you perfect, stablish, strengthen, settle you"* 1 Peter 5:10.

Perseverance – a prerequisite for a hero of faith – Matthew 10:22; *"For ye have need of patience, that, after ye have done the will of God, ye might receive the promise"* Hebrews 10:36; 12:1; *"Blessed is the man that endureth temptation: for when he is tried, he shall receive the crown of life, which the Lord hath promised to them that love him"* James 1:12.

Joseph's faith outlasted his life – *"By faith Joseph, when he died, made mention of the departing of the children of Israel; and gave commandment concerning his bones"* Hebrews 11:22; Genesis 50:25; Exodus 13:19; Joshua 24:32.

3.   List one dream you believe God has authored in your heart that you could work toward next week.

_____

Repeat this prayer out loud:

Father, I realize that You are no respecter of persons. As I've seen other men achieve their dreams, You want me to achieve my dreams as well. I lift up my dreams to You today and ask You to show me which are those You have authored and which are fantasy. Help me today to begin to achieve the dreams You have truly authored. I submit my life to You anew today and resist the enemy. In Jesus' Name. Amen.

For Further Study

God wants you to be a hero of faith – *"For there is no respect of persons with God"* Romans 2:11; *"But without faith it is impossible to please him: for he that cometh to God must believe that he is, and that he is a rewarder of them that diligently seek him"* Hebrews 11:6.

God-given dreams in God-favored men make a God-blest world – *"But thou shalt remember the Lord thy God: for it is he that giveth thee power to get wealth, that he may establish his covenant which he sware unto thy fathers"* Deuteronomy 8:18; Luke 11:9-10; *"For we are his workmanship, created in Christ Jesus unto good works, which God hath before ordained that we should walk in them"* Ephesians 2:10.

This is how God's Kingdom comes to earth through us – *"Thy kingdom come, Thy will be done, as in heaven, so in earth"* Luke 11:2.

Self Test *Lesson 1*

1. _____ are the substance of every great achievement.

2. Use the following words to fill in the blanks below:

   personality   truth   principle   reality   pattern   character

   a. _____ and _____ are synonymous.

   b. Everything God does, He does according to a _____, based on a _____ of His Kingdom.

   c. The more we base our lives upon _____ and less upon _____, the straighter our course will be.

3. God will obligate Himself to help you achieve any dream. ____ True   ____ False

4. Joseph's success came from his identification with his family and circumstances. ____ True   ____ False

5. All testing is based upon: *(circle one)*

   a. multiple choice   b. resistance   c. unhappiness

6. When Joseph told his brothers his dream, they were very happy for him. ____ True   ____ False

7. Perseverance will always outlast _____.

Keep this test for your own records.

Lesson 2

Marching to a Different Drummer

Lesson 2
Marching to a Different Drummer

A. Some men happen to influence, while others _____ to do it. *(page 19)*

    1. Good is the enemy of best. *(page 19)* ____ True ____ False

    2. What three things do men need for success? *(circle all that apply)* *(page 20)*

        a. money   c. a good wife   e. favor   g. a diploma

        b. wisdom   d. good looks   f. a high IQ   h. courage

    3. Read Luke 2:52. What increased in Jesus' life? *(page 20)*

        _____

    4. From our study, what is the definition of grace? *(page 20)*

        _____

B. Joseph's favor with God was evidenced by the fact that everything he did, God made it to _____

    _____. *(page 21)*

For Further Study

God's transcendent glory filled Joseph's life – *"And the Lord was with Joseph, and he was a prosperous man … the Lord made all that he did to prosper in his hand"* Genesis 39:2-3.

This glory helped develop his potential – Genesis 39:21-22; Romans 8:28.

God gives grace to sinners and glory to saints – *"And the glory which thou gavest me I have given them"* John 17:22; *"But where sin abounded, grace did much more abound"* Romans 5:20; 2 Corinthians 3:18; 2 Peter 1:3.

Joseph possessed favor, wisdom and courage. Favor – *"And Jesus increased in wisdom and stature, and in favour with God and man"* Luke 2:52; Favor with man – Genesis 37:3; 39:3-6; Favor with God – Genesis 39:2; *"And Pharaoh said unto Joseph, Forasmuch as God hath shown thee all this, there is none so discreet and wise as thou art"* Genesis 41:39.

1. Write out Psalm 1:1-3. _____

    _____

    _____

    _____

    _____

    _____

    _____

    _____

2. God is for prosperity and against _____. *(page 21)*

C. Read about Joseph in Genesis 39–40.

For Further Study

God's favor is always bestowed as a gift – Psalm 5:12; *"Our power is based on your favor"* Psalm 89:17 TLB; It is called unmerited favor, or God's grace – *"For by grace are ye saved through faith; and that not of yourselves: it is the gift of God"* Ephesians 2:8; 2 Timothy 1:9.

With God-given authority and ability, Joseph rose to a position of leadership everywhere he went – Genesis 39:3-6; 22-23; 40:4; 41:12-13; 39-42.

Joseph possessed favor, wisdom and courage. Wisdom – *"Wisdom gives: A long, good life Riches Honor Pleasure Peace"* Proverbs 3:16-17 TLB; *"Wisdom is the principal thing; therefore get wisdom: and with all thy getting get understanding"* Proverbs 4:7; Proverbs 3:13-26; 8:14-21. Wisdom must be sought after – Proverbs 2:1-7; 4:5; Proverbs 8:17 TLB.

We can become men of wisdom – 1 Corinthians 1:30; Colossians 2:3; *"If any of you lack wisdom, let him ask of God, that giveth to all men liberally, and upbraideth not; and it shall be given him"* James 1:5.

D. Everywhere Joseph went, he rose to a place of _____. *(page 21)*

    1. In physical life, water seeks its own level. What seeks its own level in our spiritual life? *(page 21)*

    _____

    2. As your faith rises to new levels, who must change in your life? *(page 21)*

        a. Satan   b. friends   c. spouse

    3. Who can truly keep you from achieving a new level? *(page 21)*

        a. intimate friends   b. enemies   c. employers

    4. Men tend to be intimidated by other men's _____ that are nothing more than

        _____ to justify _____. When you accept

        such philosophies, you accept the _____ upon which they are based. *(page 22)*

    5. Ministries grow to the level of their _____. *(page 23)*

E. Two things you do in life: _____ and _____. *(page 23)*

    How you leave one area of life determines how you _____ another. *(page 24)*

For Further Study

We must take time to meditate – *"This book of the law shall not depart out of thy mouth; but thou shalt meditate therein day and night … for then thou shalt make thy way prosperous, and then thou shalt have good success"* Joshua 1:8; Psalm 119:15.

Meditation is the matrix of creativity – Psalm 1:2-3; *"Meditate upon these things; give thyself wholly to them; that thy profiting may appear to all"* 1 Timothy 4:15.

Joseph possessed favor, wisdom and courage. Courage – Esther 4:8, 16. We need courage: To face reality – Psalm 51:6; To make decisions – Joshua 24:15; 2 Kings 18:21; To change – Genesis 12:1-4; 2 Chronicles 15:8; Jonah 3:4-9; To hold convictions – Nehemiah 6:10-11; Daniel 3:16-18; 6:10; Acts 4:18-20; Philippians 1:27-28; To admit wrong – Proverbs 28:13.

F. In Proverbs 4:7, we read: *(pages 24-25)*

_____ is the principle thing; therefore get _____.

G. Look up meanings, if necessary, and rewrite this statement **in your own words.** *(page 25)*

"Meditation in God's Word is the matrix of creativity."

_____

_____

1. Read out loud Joshua 1:8.

2. You can regain wealth or health, but what can you never regain? *(page 26)*

_____

H. Heroes are men who act from a need greater than _____. *(page 26)*

1. Name five reasons we need courage. *(pages 26-27)*

a. _____   c. _____   e. _____

b. _____   d. _____

For Further Study

God is the source of all – Romans 11:36; *"Every good gift and every perfect gift is from above, and cometh down from the Father of lights"* James 1:17.

Man gives money value – *"For the love of money is the root of all evil: which while some coveted after, they have erred from the faith, and pierced themselves through with many sorrows"* 1 Timothy 6:10, 17; Hebrews 12:16; 1 Peter 2:15; Jude 11.

Produce prosperity – *"And God is able to make all grace abound toward you; that ye, always having all sufficiency in all things, may abound in every good work"* 2 Corinthians 9:8.

Serve God, use money – Psalm 1:1-3; *"Man shall not live by bread alone, but by every word that proceedeth out of the mouth of God"* Matthew 4:4; Luke 12:19-21.

Be clear with debtors – *"Don't withhold repayment of your debts. Don't say 'some other time,' if you can pay now"* Proverbs 3:27-28 TLB; Romans 12:17.

Discipline the mind to keep wild thoughts from intruding into time with God – Exodus 19:12-13; 2 Corinthians 10:5.

2.   One of the hardest things for a person to admit is that he is wrong. *(page 27)*

_____ True   _____ False

I.   For God to develop the potential of your life, what do you need to give Him? *(page 27)*

_____

Practical:

1.   Reread Psalm 1:1-3.

a.   What result does God desire for your activities? _____

b.   Give a balanced perspective on prosperity for a Christian. _____

_____

For Further Study

Live within your means – *"Lazy people want much but get little, while the diligent are prospering"* Proverbs 13:4 TLB; *"Steady plodding brings prosperity; hasty speculation brings poverty"* Proverbs 21:5 TLB; Matthew 6:31-32; *"But godliness with contentment is great gain"* 1 Timothy 6:6; *"Stay away from the love of money; be satisfied with what you have"* Hebrews 13:5 TLB.

Not everyone lives at the same level of faith – Romans 12:3-6; 2 Peter 1:1.

A ministry grows to the level of its leader – Matthew 10:24-25.

Retaining associations with those who will not grow can frustrate and discourage growth in our own lives – *"Be ye not unequally yoked together with unbelievers"* 2 Corinthians 6:14.

We can be intimidated by other men's philosophies which are rationalizations to justify failures. When you accept such philosophies, you accept their failures – Psalm 1:1; Colossians 2:8.

2. Read Psalm 5:12.

    a. To whom does God give favor? _____

    b. Do you qualify? ____ Yes ____ No

    c. If you pray for forgiveness and cleansing according to 1 John 1:9, will you be forgiven and cleansed? ____ Yes ____ No

    d. If you are forgiven and cleansed, are you righteous? ____ Yes ____ No

    e. Does God want to favor you? ____ Yes ____ No

3. Look through the first chapters of Proverbs and list some benefits of wisdom.

_____

_____

Repeat this prayer out loud:

Father, in Jesus' Name, You've called me to be an overcomer. I thank You now for the favor, the wisdom and the courage to be all that You've made me to be. I will not let others create a smaller vision for my life than the one You've put in my spirit. I will pursue excellence in my tasks as You would have me to do. I will not allow my dreams to perish because of wrong associations. I will fulfill Your call on my life as a husband, as a businessman and as a man. Amen.

For Further Study

God wants us to grow from glory to glory so we can fulfill our dream – *"But we all, with open face beholding as in a glass the glory of the Lord, are changed into the same image from glory to glory, even as by the Spirit of the Lord"* 2 Corinthians 3:18.

Don't let anyone's unbelief, rejection of truth or refusal to grow stop your dream – Numbers 13:30.

Grow with God – *"And now, brethren, I commend you to God, and to the word of his grace, which is able to build you up, and to give you an inheritance among all them which are sanctified"* Acts 20:32; Grow in grace – *"But grow in grace, and in the knowledge of our Lord and Saviour Jesus Christ. To him be glory both now and for ever"* 2 Peter 3:18; Grow in truth – *"Buy the truth, and sell it not; also wisdom, and instruction, and understanding"* Proverbs 23:23.

Self Test *Lesson 2*

1. What is the difference between a follower and a leader?

   _____.

   _____.

2. What three things do we all need to succeed?

   a. _____

   b. _____

   c. _____

3. What is one meaning of "grace"?

   _____

4. Poverty is a Godly, biblical principle that all God's people must embrace.   _____ True   _____ False

5. You will always grow only as far as the level of your _____.

6. What must change as you grow to new levels in life? _____

7. What are the two basic things we do in life?

   a. _____   b. _____

8. What is one of the hardest things for men to do? *(a first step toward maturity)*

   _____

9. What is the definition of a hero?

   _____.

Keep this test for your own records.

Lesson 3

Your Life Has Potential &
Convert Your Negatives to Positives

Lesson 3

Your Life Has Potential &
Convert Your Negatives to Positives

I.   Your Life Has Potential (Chapter 3)

    A.   Exchange is the _____ of life. *(page 31)*

        1.   God makes something from nothing. *(page 31)*   ____ True   ____ False

        2.   Write out Hebrews 11:3.

        _____

        _____

        _____

        3.   According to this verse, "things" are made from what is not seen. *(page 31)*

        ____ True   ____ False

For Further Study

Something is not made from nothing but from things not seen – *"The worlds were framed by the word of God, so that things which are seen were not made of things which do appear"* Hebrews 11:3.

The eternal that cannot be seen is far more important than the temporal that can be seen – Luke 9:12-17; *"While we look not at the things which are seen, but at the things which are not seen: for the things which are seen are temporal; but the things which are not seen are eternal"* 2 Corinthians 4:18.

Exchange is the process for the development of potential – Luke 19:12, 13, 15.

Jesus came in His righteousness and became identified with our sins so that we could become identified with His righteousness – *"For he hath made him to be sin for us, who knew no sin; that we might be made the righteousness of God in him"* 2 Corinthians 5:21.

4. The true value of anything is _____, not _____. *(page 32)*

5. Marriage is the closest thing to a _____ or _____ there is in this life. *(page 33)*

6. What do we exchange for Christ's righteousness at Calvary? *(page 33)* _____

7. Use "righteousness" and "identified" to complete this sentence: *(page 33)*

   Jesus came in His _____ and became _____ with

   our sins so that we, through repentance and faith, could become _____

   with His _____.

8. Write out James 1:22. _____

   _____

For Further Study

Calvary holds only *potential* for salvation, until you develop it by exchanging your sins for God's righteousness – *"To wit, that God was in Christ, reconciling the world unto himself, not imputing their trespasses unto them … we pray you in Christ's stead, be ye reconciled to God"* 2 Corinthians 5:19-20; 6:1-2.

Spiritual overcomers – Matthew 7:21; James 1:22-25; *"And he that overcometh, and keepth my works unto the end, to him will I give power over the nations … To him that overcometh will I grant to sit with me in my throne, even as I also overcame, and am set down with my Father in his throne"* Revelations 2:26; 3:21.

Overcomers begin with what they have; others moan for what they don't have – John 6:5-11.

Faith is believing that what you cannot see will come to pass – *"Now faith is the substance of things hoped for, the evidence of things not seen"* Hebrews 11:1.

B. Where do successful men begin? *(page 34)* _____

What do they begin with? *(page 34)* _____

C. Read about Joseph in Genesis 41-42.

D. Using the words "faith" and "fear" fill in the following: *(page 35)*

_____ and _____ both attract. _____ and _____ is believing that what you

cannot see will come to pass. _____ attracts the positive; _____ attracts the negative.

Name two things that Joseph refused to be limited by. *(page 37)*

_____

_____

II. Convert Your Negatives to Positives (Chapter 4)

A. God ends everything on the _____. *(page 39)*

For Further Study

Fear is believing that what you cannot see will come to pass – *"For the thing which I greatly feared is come upon me, and that which I was afraid of is come unto me"* Job 3:25.

God never ends anything on a negative – *"God turned into good what you meant for evil"* Genesis 50:20 TLB.

God created Adam perfect in his humanity, then God rested – Genesis 1:27, 31; 2:2.

Peace has always been the umpire of doing the will of God – *"And let the peace (soul harmony that comes) from the Christ rule (act as umpire continually) in your hearts [deciding and settling with finality all questions that arise in your minds]"* Colossians 3:15 AMP.

The characteristics of the kingdom emanate from the character of the king – Proverbs 29:2; Hosea 4:9; 1 Thessalonians 1:6, 7.

B. Peace is the _____ for knowing the will of God. *(page 40)*

C. When Adam sinned, all human nature was changed from _____ to _____.
    (page 40)

    1. Everything in life must be converted from _____ to _____. *(page 40)*

    2. We are _____ by nature. *(page 41)*

D. The characteristics of the kingdom emanate from the _____. *(page 41)*

    1. Sin is always _____. *(page 42)*

    2. Name some ways that people need to convert. *(page 42)* _____

    _____

E. What is the atmosphere for miracles? *(page 43)* _____

For Further Study

All characteristics of God's Kingdom are positive.

Light	– Isaiah 60:19; 1 Peter 2:9; 1 John 1:5; Revelations 21:23
Life	– John 10:10; 11:25; 17:2; 20:31
Love	– Romans 5:8; 1 John 3:1; 4:8
Truth	– Deuteronomy 32:4; Isaiah 65:16; John 14:6
Obedience	– Daniel 7:27; Matthew 5:19; Luke 11:2

All characteristics of Satan's kingdom are negative.

Darkness	– Ephesians 6:12; Colossians 1:13
Death	– John 10:10; Revelations 20:14
Lust	– John 8:44
Lying	– John 8:44
Disobedience	– Ephesians 2:2

F. Fill in the blank with the letter of the word that matches the following phrases: *(pages 44-45)*

    ____ 1. the basis of life   a. repentance

    ____ 2. sets in when communication stops   b. reconciliation

    ____ 3. ultimate end of abnormality   c. communication

    ____ 4. a way to stop death   d. death

    ____ 5. pivotal point between ruin and reconciliation   e. abnormality

G. Read Luke 15:11-24.

    1. What is the pattern of the prodigal son? *(page 45)* _____

      _____

    2. When the prodigal broke off communication from his father, his life became: *(page 45)*

      a. better   b. livelier   c. abnormal

    3. Change came when the prodigal: *(page 45)*

      a. repented   b. wrote a book   c. heard the right sermon

For Further Study

We are conditioned to failure and subject to sin – Romans 5:18-19; therefore, we must be converted in all areas of our life – Romans 12:2; 2 Corinthians 3:18.

Expectancy is the atmosphere for miracles – Acts 3:4-5. Unbelief stifles miracles – Mark 6:5-6.

Jesus gives peace – John 14:27; Philippians 4:7; but every area of life must be yielded to the Spirit of God – Romans 8:6; and sin renounced – 1 Peter 3:11, 12; to find the peace of God – Psalms 22:5; 28:7; 85:8; Isaiah 12:2; 26:3; John 16:33; Colossians 3:15.

Everything God made is good – Genesis 1:31; Psalm 139:15; Man makes good things negative – Genesis 3:17; Sin desires to enslave – Hebrews 3:13.

When communication stops, abnormality sets in – John 16:6 then 15:6; Reconciliation brings renewed communication – 2 Corinthians 5:20-6:2.

Practical:

1. Look up Job 3:25 and discuss the nature of faith and fear.

   _____

   _____

2. Read: *"[You were obedient to and under the control of] the [demon] spirit that still constantly works in the sons of disobedience [the careless, the rebellious, and the unbelieving, who go against the purposes of God]"* Ephesians 2:2b AMP.

   Considering our study, what does this verse mean to you?

   _____

   _____

Repeat this prayer out loud:

Lord God, thank You for creating my life to end on a positive. I want to exchange my sins today for Christ's righteousness and become identified anew with the life of Christ. I reject fear and, by faith, ask You, Lord, to make me a success. I commit to start right where I am with what I have. I trust You to take what I submit to You and turn all my negatives into positives. In the Name of Jesus, I pray. Amen.

For Further Study

Repentance is the pivotal point between ruin and reconciliation – Luke 15:11-24; Acts 3:19.
Communication by spirit – Proverbs 23:7; *"A man with hate in his heart may sound pleasant enough, but don't believe him; for he is cursing you in his heart"* Proverbs 26:24-26 TLB.
Prayer produces intimacy – Acts 2:42-44.
Reliable communication – Mark 4:11-12, 23-24
Distortion in the hearers – John 12:28-29; Deliberate distortion – Jeremiah 9:5; Romans 16:18
Communication with others – *"Wherefore, my beloved brethren, let every man be swift to hear, slow to speak, slow to wrath"* James 1:19; With wives – *"Husbands, in the same way be considerate as you live with your wives, and treat them with respect"* 1 Peter 3:7 NIV; With children – *"And ye fathers, provoke not your children to wrath: but bring them up in the nurture and admonition of the Lord"* Ephesians 6:4.
Communicate your love – *"Open rebuke is better than hidden love"* Proverbs 27:5 TLB; *"Let us not love in word, neither in tongue; but in deed and in truth"* 1 John 3:18.

Self Test *Lesson 3*

1. What is the "process" of life? _____

2. What is the "basis" of life? _____

3. God made everything out of: *(circle one)*

   a. unseen substances   b. nothing   c. sticks and stones

4. The definition of both faith and fear is believing that something you cannot see will come to pass.

   _____ True   _____ False

   a. Faith attracts the _____.

   b. Fear attracts the _____.

5. God ends everything on a _____.

6. What is the "umpire" for doing the will of God? *(circle one)*

   a. faith   b. love   c. peace

7. **In your own words,** what changed in human nature when Adam sinned?

   _____

   _____

8. _____ is natural to negative human nature.

9. From what come the characteristics of a kingdom? _____

10. What is the atmosphere for miracles? *(circle one)*

    a. worship   b. expectancy   c. prayer

11. What is the pivotal point between ruin and reconciliation? *(circle one)*

    a. rebellion   b. repentance   c. restoration

Keep this test for your own records.

Lesson 4

Character Building Blocks &
Image, Image on My Mind

Lesson 4
Character Building Blocks &
Image, Image on My Mind

I.   Character Building Blocks (Chapter 5)

A.   Write out 2 Timothy 2:2. _____

_____

_____

1.   If men are faithful, God will add the _____. *(page 50)*

2.   Fishermen don't clean their fish before they catch them. **In your own words,** what spiritual principle

does this illustrate? _____

_____

3.   Some people are better by nature than others are by grace. *(page 51)* _____ True _____ False

4.   The world puts a premium on: *(circle one) (page 51)*

a. character   b. humor   c. talent

For Further Study

Character is always more important than talent – *"And the things that thou hast heard of me among many witnesses, the same commit thou to faithful men, who shall be able to teach others also"* 2 Timothy 2:2; Proverbs 22:1.

Humanity tends to major on externals rather then the internal – *"Woe unto you, scribes and Pharisees, hypocrites! for ye make clean the outside of the cup and of the platter, but within they are full of extortion and excess"* Matthew 23:25-28; John 7:24.

The world puts a premium on talent, not character – 2 Corinthians 5:12.

A right relationship to God enables us to receive revelation – John 14:21, 23.

Crisis builds character – Genesis 50:20; Psalm 105:17-22. Crisis is normal to life – John 16:33. Crisis takes us from the transient to the permanent – 1 Peter 1:6-7.

B. What has most to do with hearing from God? *(circle one)* *(page 52)*

a. maturity   b. relationship   c. age

C. In what way is food like knowledge? *(page 52)*

_____

D. What continually happened in Joseph's life? *(page 52)*

a. easy living   b. weight loss   c. crisis

Fill in the sentences below with the following words: *(pages 52-54)*

authority   external   transient   glory   sorrow

crisis   internal   permanent   accountability

1. _____ is normal to life.

2. Crisis takes us from a _____ to a _____ situation.

3. _____ is life's greatest teacher.

4. God recreated Joseph's life by His transcendent _____.

5. The value of anything is always _____, not _____.

6. God never gives _____ without _____.

For Further Study

Sorrow is one of life's greatest teachers – *"It is good for me that I have been afflicted; that I might learn thy stautes"* Psalm 119:71; *"Sorrow is better than laughter: for by sadness of the countenance the heart is made better"* Ecclesiastes 7:3. Joseph's submission was not to the circumstances but to the God of transcendent glory – *"Even God, who quickeneth the dead, and calleth those things which be not as though they were"* Romans 4:17; 8:28; Philippians 1:12, 13, 19.

God takes your life as it is, makes it something and brings glory to His Name – *"And I was with thee whithersoever thou wentest, and have cut off all thine enemies out of thy sight, and have made thee a great name, like unto the name of the great men that are in the earth"* 2 Samuel 7:9.

Develop a genuine desire for God – Psalms 42:1, 2; 63:1, 8; 84:2; Jeremiah 29:13; Hebrews 11:6.

E.   When you invest in a company, what are you really investing in? *(page 55)*

_____

Which is more important: character or talent? *(page 55)* _____

II.   Image, Image on My Mind (Chapter 6)

A.   One of the most powerful things you can do in life is create an _____. The next most powerful

thing you can do is _____ it. *(page 57)*

1.   We are motivated to become _____. *(page 57)*

2.   Read Proverbs 23:7 and rewrite the first phrase using *your own name*.

_____

B.   Two-thirds of our lifetime impressions are made before we are what age? *(page 57)* _____

1.   Adult problems more often than not stem from our _____. *(page 58)*

2.   Images have potential for good or harm. *(page 58)*   ____ True   ____ False

3.   Parents create images in children's minds. *(pages 58-59)*   ____ True   ____ False

---

For Further Study

Anger toward sin and a desire to reprove it – *"I will set no wicked thing before mine eyes: I hate the work of them that turn aside; it shall not cleave to me"* Psalm 101:3.

Willingness to face persecution rather then capitulate to sin – Hebrews 12:3-4; *"Forasmuch then as Christ hath suffered for us in the flesh, arm yourselves likewise with the same mind: for he that hath suffered in the flesh hath ceased from sin"* 1 Peter 4:1.

God requires faithfulness. He will provide you with ability – 1 Corinthians. 4:2; 1 Timothy 1:12; 2 Timothy 2:2.

God never gives authority without accountability – *"For unto whomsoever much is given, of him shall be much required"* Luke 12:48; Matthew 18:23; Luke 19:15; Romans 14:12.

Christlikeness is the ultimate good that God's transcendent glory works to produce – Romans 8:29; 2 Corinthians 3:18.

C. Name Satan's two major weapons. *(page 60)* _____

    1. Counselors tear down old _____ and reconstruct new ones. *(page 60)*

    2. **In your own words,** name some ways we create poor images of God in children's minds.

        _____

    3. How did Jesus create images? *(page 61)* _____

D. Write "T" for True and "F" for False. *(pages 61-62)*

    ____ Salvation is an end in itself.

    ____ The day you get married is only the beginning.

    ____ True Christians never experience problems after salvation.

    ____ Changing an image changes behavior.

    ____ You can never change your feelings, just accept them.

    ____ Your image of yourself is more important than your image of God.

For Further Study

Your value is in the Christlikeness of your character – *"But in a great house there are not only vessels of gold and of silver, but also of wood and of earth; and some to honour, and some to dishonour. If a man therefore purge himself from these, he shall be a vessel unto honour, sanctified, and meet for the master's use, and prepared unto every good work"* 2 Timothy 2:20-21.

Images have a powerful influence on our lives – Proverbs 23:7; Titus 1:15.

One of the most important things you can do in life is create an image – Psalm 115:4-8.

The next most powerful thing you can do is destroy it – Numbers 33:52.

Joseph's God-given dream established an image in his mind of who he was and who he was to become – Genesis 37:5-11.

E.   Write out a definition of the "Saul Syndrome." *(page 64)*

_____

_____

_____

F.   Read about Joseph in Genesis 43–44.

Practical:

1.   Read: *"Casting down imaginations, and every high thing that exalteth itself against the knowledge of God, and bringing into captivity every thought to the obedience of Christ"* 2 Corinthians 10:5. What does this verse have to do with what you've just studied?

_____

_____

For Further Study

Our early experiences create images that have great influence – 2 Timothy 1:5; *"From a child thou hast known the holy scriptures"* 2 Timothy 3:15.

Teach children to discern right from wrong – *"Train up a child in the way he should go: and when he is old, he will not depart from it"* Proverbs 22:6.

Our images must be renewed – 1 Samuel 17:32; 2 Corinthians 5:17; *"Be renewed in the spirit of your mind"* Ephesians 4:22-23.

God wants us to know Him personally, intimately – *"Draw nigh to God, and he will draw nigh to you"* James 4:8.

Our image of God is not from doctrines of men – *"That your faith should not stand in the wisdom of men, but in the power of God"* 1 Corinthians 2:5; *"Beware lest any man spoil you through philosophy and vain deceit, after the tradition of men ... and not after Christ"* Colossians 2:8.

2. A church deacon is excited about starting a new Sunday night program. The pastor wants to stop Sunday evening services to promote family worship in the home. What should each of them do?

_____

_____

Repeat this prayer out loud:

Father, in the Name of Jesus, I set myself in agreement with Your Word to become a faithful man. I cast down vain imaginations and everything that raises itself in my mind against the image of Jesus Christ. Please help me see how You see me and set me free from old, negative images. Amen.

For Further Study

We can be seriously restricted by others' images of ourselves – 1 Samuel 17:28-29; *"And they said one to another, Behold, this dreamer cometh. Come now therefore, and let us slay him, and cast him into some pit ... and we shall see what will become of his dreams"* Genesis 37:19-20.

We must seek images from God, not man – *"And be not conformed to this world: but be ye transformed by the renewing of your mind, that ye may prove what is that good, and acceptable, and perfect, will of God"* Romans 12:2; 1 Corinthians 6:20; 2 Corinthians 3:18; 1 Peter 1:18-21.

What should really count in your life is not what you or others think, but what God thinks – *"How can ye believe, which receive honour one of another, and seek not the honour that cometh from God only?"* John 5:44.

Self Test *Lesson 4*

1. What type of men does God commit to? *(circle one)*

   a. able men   b. wise men   c. faithful men   d. talented men

2. For God to use you, you need one major prerequisite: _____

3. Hearing from God has much to do with the age of the individual. ____ True ____ False

4. What common circumstance in Joseph's life is common to life itself? _____

5. What is one of life's greatest teachers? _____ _____

6. God never gives authority without _____.

7. The real value of anything is always: *(circle one)*

   a. internal   b. external   c. fraternal

8. One of the most powerful things you can do in life is create: *(circle one)*

   a. a ministry   b. a newsletter   c. an image

9. Satan's two major weapons in his arsenal are:

   a. _____   b. _____

10. Why is television so powerful?

    _____

11. What is a primary way to change your behavior?

    _____

Keep this test for your own records.

Lesson 5

The Way Up Is Down

Lesson 5
The Way Up Is Down

A. We are qualified to lead only _____. *(page 67)*

  1. Fill in the blank: *"And whosoever of you will be the chiefest, shall be* _____ *of all"* Mark 10:44.

    Name two men from the Bible who were great because of serving others. *(pages 68-69)*

    _____ _____

  2. The more we serve, the _____ we become. *(page 67)*

  3. A father's greatness with his family is based on his _____. *(page 68)*

B. Give definitions for the following words: *(page 68)*

  1. Servitude: _____

  2. Serving: _____

  3. Love: _____

  4. Lust: _____

For Further Study

We are qualified to lead only to the degree we are willing to serve – *"Whosoever will be great among you, let him be your minister; And whosoever will be chief among you, let him be your servant"* Matthew 20:25-28; *"I am among you as he that serveth"* Luke 22:25-27; John 13:13-16.

The more we serve, the greater we become – *"But he that is greatest among you shall be your servant"* Matthew 23:11. Our care for others is the measure of our greatness – Matthew 24:45-47; Luke 9:47-48.

A father's greatness with his family is based on his care for them – *"For I know him, that he will command his children and his household after him, and they shall keep the way of the Lord"* Genesis 18:19; Ephesians 6:4.

Serving is not servitude – *"Let this mind be in you, which was also in Christ Jesus: Who, being in the form of God … But made himself of no reputation, and took upon him the form of a servant"* Philippians 2:5-9.

C. Write out 1 John 2:16 then circle the three main life motivations (the three major categories of sin).

_____

_____

_____

D. Read about Joseph in Genesis 45–46.

E. What is better than practicing what you preach? *(page 71)*

_____

F. Name and explain the four levels we can live on. *(pages 71-72)*

1. _____: Life's _____ of knowledge.

2. Knowledge: Comes from the accumulation of _____.

3. _____: The ability to put _____.

4. _____: _____.

Leadership comes from this level.

G. Every leader is limited by three things in his life. *(page 72)*

1. The _____ of his own mind.

2. The _____ of his own character.

3. The _____ upon which he is building his own life.

For Further Study

Love is a characteristic of God's Kingdom – *"Herein is love, not that we loved God, but that he loved us, and sent his Son to be the propitiation for our sins"* 1 John 4:9-10.

Lust is a characteristic of Satan's kingdom – *"Ye are of your father the devil, and the lusts of your father ye will do"* John 8:44; Proverbs 27:20; *"For all that is in the world, the lust of the flesh, and the lust of the eyes, and the pride of life, is not of the Father, but is of the world"* 1 John 2:16.

Leadership has the potential for good or harm – *"When the righteous are in authority, the people rejoice: but when the wicked beareth rule, the people mourn"* Proverbs 29:2; 1 Chronicles 28:8-9; Ecclesiastes 10:5.

Four levels we can live on:

Assumption: life's lowest level of knowledge – Matthew 13:19; Isaiah 5:13; Knowledge: knowing the facts but not living them – Ezekiel 33:30-32; James 1:22-24; Ability: able to act on knowledge, but we don't make it a part of our life – Matthew 7:26; Practice: the highest learning level – Matthew 7:24

H.   A man's private life has nothing to do with his public performance. *(page 72)* _____ True   _____ False

   1.   Good leadership requires: *(circle all that apply)* *(page 72)*

      a. intelligence   c. good looks   e. knowledge   g. education

      b. character   d. sternness   f. good health   h. principles

   2.   *"The husbandman that laboureth must be first partaker of the fruits"* 2 Timothy 2:6. This illustrates what leadership principle? *(page 73)*

     _____

     _____

   3.   Public _____ must follow private _____. *(page 73)*

I.   Give your own example of "transposition." *(page 73)*

     _____

Write in the letter of the word that matches the phrases below: *(pages 73, 75)*

_____ 1. what to preach   a. intercession

_____ 2. what to practice (live)   b. Word

_____ 3. comes from agreement   c. holiness

_____ 4. what God wants you to be   d. a success

_____ 5. what you might be   e. consecration

_____ 6. get a higher degree of this   f. a disappointment

_____ 7. get a greater understanding of this   g. power

For Further Study

Limitations of leadership: The knowledge of the mind – *"I have more understanding than all my teachers: for thy testimonies are my meditation"* Psalm 119:99; *"Study to show thyself approved unto God, a workman that needeth not to be ashamed, rightly dividing the word of truth"* 2 Timothy 2:15; The worth of the character – *"If a man therefore purge himself from these, he shall be a vessel unto honour, sanctified, and meet for the master's use, and prepared unto every good work"* 2 Timothy 2:21; Luke 16:10-12; 1 Corinthians 4:2; The principles upon which to build the life – *"Get wisdom, get understanding: forget it not; neither decline from the words of my mouth. Forsake her not, and she shall preserve thee: love her and she shall keep thee. Wisdom is the principal thing; therefore get wisdom: and with all thy getting get understanding"* Proverbs 4:5-8; Psalm 119:133.

Practical:

1. The greatest companies are those who serve the most people. Give some examples of people or organizations that have become great through serving.

    _____

    In what areas can you become better at serving others? _____

    _____

2. Many of today's leaders say their private life doesn't affect their public life. Do you agree or disagree?
    _____ Why? _____

3. What does it mean to you to "preach the Word and practice your consecration"? Think through some doctrines of the Word you can "preach" or teach others as absolutes and other doctrines that are part of your consecration, personal theology or denominational teachings.

    PREACH   **PRACTICE**

    _____   _____

    _____   _____

Repeat this prayer out loud:

Father, in Jesus' Name, I choose this day to be one of Your victories. Therefore, I recognize the need to be an example in serving. You've ordained that I be one of Your leaders, particularly in my family. Therefore, I will lead in love and bring glory to You. Amen.

For Further Study

Leadership requires knowledge, character and principles – *"For Ezra had prepared his heart to seek the law of the Lord, and to do it, and to teach in Israel statutes and judgments"* Ezra 7:10.

There must be private renunciation of sin – Luke 4:12-15.

The leader must first practice what he wants others to do before they follow him – *"Be thou an example of the believers, in word, in conversation (manner of life), in charity, in spirit, in faith, in purity"* 1 Timothy 4:12; 1 Peter 5:3.

Taking up, not giving up, is the issue of leadership – *"If any man will come after me, let him deny himself, and take up his cross, and follow me. For whosoever will save his life shall lose it: and whosoever will lose his life for my sake will find it"* Matthew 16:24-25; Matthew 10:38-39; Luke 9:23.

The place of agreement is the place of power – Matthew 18:19.

Joseph's entire life was one of serving others – Genesis 39:3-5, 22; 40:4.

Self Test *Lesson 5*

1. Our willingness to _____ qualifies us to lead others.

2. The measure of our greatness is seen in how we _____ for others.

3. What is the major difference between serving and servitude?

   a. _____

   b. _____

4. What is the major difference between lust and love?

   a. _____

   b. _____

5. Lust is a characteristic of the kingdom of _____.

6. What is the lowest level of living? _____

7. Every leader is limited by three things in his life. What are they?

   a. _____

   b. _____

   c. _____

8. What must happen before we, as men or ministers, can publicly denounce sin?

   _____

9. Preach the _____ ; practice your _____.

10. The place of agreement is the place of _____.

Keep this test for your own records.

Lesson 6

Confession Is Good for You &
It's in Your Mouth

Lesson 6
Confession Is Good for You &
It's in Your Mouth

I. Confession Is Good for You (Chapter 8)

    A. You are committed to what you _____. *(page 78)*

        1. According to Romans 10:10, how do we confirm our salvation? _____

        2. The confirmation of our _____ is established by the _____ of our mouth. *(page 78)*

    B. You can't do _____'s part. _____ will not do your part. *(page 80)*

        1. Repentance must be balanced by _____. *(page 80)*

        2. Believing must be balanced by _____. *(page 80)*

        3. Tenderness must be balanced by _____. *(page 81)*

        4. Balance is the _____ to life. *(page 81)*

        5. Confess out _____. Confess in _____. *(page 81)*

For Further Study

Confession confirms our faith – *"The word is nigh thee, even in thy mouth, and in thy heart: that is, the word of faith, which we preach; That if thou shalt confess with thy mouth the Lord Jesus, and shalt believe in thine heart that God hath raised him from the dead, thou shalt be saved. For with the heart man believeth unto righteousness; and with the mouth confession is made unto salvation"* Romans 10:8-10.

Gratitude and appreciation are forms of praise – *"Let the peace of God rule in your hearts ... and be ye thankful"* Colossians 3:15.

Praise brings God into your circumstances and relationships – *"But thou art holy, O thou that inhabitest the praises of Israel"* Psalm 22:3.

Confession of sin must be balanced by faith – *"Testifying both to the Jews, and also to the Greeks, repentance toward God, and faith toward our Lord Jesus Christ"* Acts 20:21; Hebrews 6:1.

C. Read Hebrews 1:3.

    1.   All God's creative power is in His _____. *(page 81)*

    2.   Life is composed of your _____ and constructed by your _____. *(page 81)*

    3.   My life is the sum total of my _____. *(page 81)*

    4.   Words spoken to me have no creative power. *(page 82)* _____ True _____ False

    5.   Read Matthew 12:36-37 and rewrite it **in your own words.**

    _____

    _____

    _____

    _____

D. Read about Joseph in Genesis 47–48.

For Further Study

Confess out your sin – *"If we confess our sins, he is faithful and just to forgive us our sins, and to cleanse us from all unrighteousness"* 1 John 1:9.

Confess in your righteousness – *"Let the redeemed of the Lord say so, whom he hath redeemed from the hand of the enemy"* Psalm 107:2.

What you believe is what you confess – *"A good man out of the good treasure of his heart bringeth forth that which is good; and an evil man out of the evil treasures of his heart bringeth forth that which is evil: for out of the abundance of the heart his mouth speaketh"* Luke 6:45.

Life is composed of your choices and constructed by your words – *"Whoso keepeth his mouth and his tongue keepeth his soul from troubles"* Proverbs 21:23; Proverbs 15:4.

E. God spoke, and His Word went forth to _____ what His Word commanded. *(page 83)*

In what way does your own word work? _____

Is it important to confess your dreams?   ____ Yes   ____ No

II. It's in Your Mouth (Chapter 9)

A. Write two definitions of a hypocrite. *(pages 85-86)* _____

_____

_____

_____

1. What are some common factors that prevent people today from identifying with Jesus? *(pages 86)*

a. _____

b. _____

c. _____

For Further Study

Words are the expression of our life – *"Out of the abundance of the heart his mouth speaketh"* Matthew 12:34-35.
We are the sum total of all the words we have spoken or that were spoken to us in our lives – *"Death and life are in the power of the tongue: and they that love it shall eat the fruit thereof"* Proverbs 18:21.
God upholds all things by the word of His power – *"Who being the brightness of his glory, and the express image of his person, and upholding all things by the word of his power"* Hebrews 1:3.
Every word spoken has power to create in the positive or in the negative – Mark 11:23; *"Thou art snared with the words of thy mouth, thou art taken with the words of thy mouth"* Proverbs 6:2; Matthew 12:37.
Hypocrisy – a "mask wearer" – *"Beware ye of the leaven of the Pharisees, which is hypocrisy"* Luke 12:1.

2.   You are committed to what you _____. *(page 87)*

3.   Why would a man not want to recite marriage vows? *(pages 87-88)*

_____

B.   Is a man a real man if he goes to church but won't confess he's a Christian at work? *(pages 88-89)*

____ Yes   ____ No

1.   Confession has the potential to do good or _____. *(page 89)*

2.   Give two examples of Biblical men who made rash vows or confessions and briefly explain. *(page 89)*

_____

_____

_____

_____

For Further Study

Saying one thing, living in another manner – *"The scribes and the Pharisees sit in Moses' seat ... do not ye after their works: for they say, and do not"* Matthew 23:2-3; Jeremiah 7:9-10.
Believing one thing in the heart, saying another with the mouth – *"Ye hypocrites, well did Esaias (Isaiah) prophesy of you, saying, This people draweth nigh unto me with their mouth, and honoureth me with their lips; but their heart is far from me"* Matthew 15:7-8.
Moral cowardice: one who does not want to confess Christ publicly, because he does not want to commit himself to living the life – *"Nevertheless among the chief rulers also many believed on him; but because of the Pharisees they did not confess him, lest they should be put out of the synagogue: For they loved the praise of men more then the praise of God"* John 12:42-43.

C.   Name two feelings that can stop a man from receiving what God has for him. *(page 90)*

_____   _____

    1.   Receiving and confessing is as important as _____. *(page 90)*

    2.   Write out Psalm 84:11. _____

_____

_____

    3.   Can you earn anything from God? *(page 91)* ____ Yes ____ No

Practical:

    1.   Read out loud 1 John 1:9. Have you confessed your sins? _____ Has God forgiven you? _____

Why do you think people have trouble accepting God's forgiveness? _____

_____

For Further Study

Confession has potential for good or harm – *"For by thy words thou shalt be justified, and by thy words thou shalt be condemned"* Matthew 12:37. Example: a rash vow – *"When thou vowest a vow unto God, defer not to pay it; for he hath no pleasure in fools: pay that which thou hast vowed. Better is it that thou shouldest not vow, than that thou shouldest vow and not pay. Suffer not thy mouth to cause thy flesh to sin"* Ecclesiastes 5:4-6; Jephthah's vow – Judges 11:30-36.

Confession of our worthiness in Christ – *"For he hath made him to be sin for us, who knew no sin; that we might be made the righteousness of God in him"* 2 Corinthians 5:21.

Based on grace, not works – *"For by grace are ye saved through faith; and that not of yourselves: it is the gift of God"* Ephesians 2:8; Titus 3:5.

2.   What do you confess on a regular basis: positive words or negative?
     For the next week, keep a piece of paper in your pocket and put down a mark each time you use negative words, whether in truth or joking, to or about the following people:

     wife   children   subordinate(s)   employer   colleague(s)   church leadership

3.   A man with a college degree and talent for business works in a warehouse and complains everyday that he isn't where he's capable of being. On a separate sheet, draw up a plan for what that man should do.

Repeat this prayer out loud:

Father, I receive today all that Christ has done for me. I set my mouth in agreement with Your Word, to confess for myself, my family and everyone I know only the words that are pleasing to You. Please seal this lesson in my heart and mind to keep me aware of the words I choose. In Jesus' Name, I ask. Amen.

For Further Study

Trust God to meet your needs – *"But my God shall supply all your need according to his riches in glory by Christ Jesus"* Philippians 4:19; *"The Lord is my Shepard; I shall not want"* Psalm 23:1.
Receive great things from God – *"Now unto him that is able to do exceeding abundantly above all that we ask or think, according to the power that worketh in us"* Ephesians 3:20.
Receiving is as important as believing.
If, after believing, you cannot receive, you nullify your believing – *"What things soever ye desire, when ye pray, believe that ye receive them, and ye shall have them"* Mark 11:24.
Believe God for great things, then receive those things from God – *"It is your Father's good pleasure to give you the kingdom"* Luke 12:32.

Self Test *Lesson 6*

1. A Kingdom principle is that you are committed to what you confess.   _____ True   _____ False

2. We confess _____ sin, and confess _____ righteousness.

3. Match the following:

    _____ Repentance must be balanced by   a. the key to life

    _____ Believing must be balanced by   b. toughness

    _____ Tenderness must be balanced by   c. receiving

    _____ Balance is   d. faith

4. Life is composed of your _____ and constructed by your _____.

5. God wants us to speak out or confess our dreams.   _____ True   _____ False

6. What's a definition of a "hypocrite"?

    _____

    _____

7. Jesus is called the "Word" of God in human form, the expression of God on earth. What form do your words take? If put in human form, what would it look like?

    _____

    _____

    _____

Keep this test for your own records.

Lesson 7

Master Your Passion

Lesson 7
Master Your Passion

A. _____ your _____ or your _____ will _____ you. *(page 93)*

    1.   What are some passions that control men? *(page 93)*

          _____

    2.   How did Joseph develop his character to control his passions? *(page 93)*

          _____

B. "Snap decisions" are made on the spur of the moment and have nothing to do with a man's private life. *(page 94)* _____ True _____ False

    1.   How do you develop character that helps you withstand spur-of-the-moment temptation? *(page 94)*

          _____

          _____

    2.   What is the criteria of holiness? *(page 94)* _____

    3.   Not meditating on God's Word is the sin of _____. *(pages 94-95)*

    4.   Decision always translates into _____. *(page 95)*

    5.   What is the test of true character? *(page 95)*

          _____

For Further Study

Everyone has a master passion – *"This I say then, Walk in the Spirit, and ye shall not fulfil the lust of the flesh. For the flesh lusteth against the Spirit, and the Spirit against the flesh: and these are contrary the one to the other: so that ye cannot do the things that ye would"* Galatians 5:16-17; Example: Sex – *"Flee also youthful lusts: but follow righteousness"* 2 Timothy 2:22; Power – *"And the devil said unto him, All this power will I give thee, and the glory of them"* Luke 4:5-8; Pleasure – *"Lovers of pleasures more than lovers of God"* 2 Timothy 3:4.

Spur-of-the-moment decisions are grounded in character – *"Keep thy heart with all diligence; for out of it are the issues of life"* Proverbs 4:23.

The true measure of character is what you think about when you are alone – Ezekiel 8:12; *"Finally, brethren, whatsoever things are true, whatsoever things are honest, whatsoever things are just, whatsoever things are pure, whatsoever things are lovely, whatsoever things are of good report; if there be any virtue, and if there be any praise, think on these things"* Philippians 4:8.

C. There isn't anything Satan doesn't want to _____ because he wants to take the place of _____. *(pages 95-96)*

    1. Read: *"But every man is tempted, when he is drawn away of his own lust, and enticed. Then when lust hath conceived, it bringeth forth sin: and sin, when it is finished, bringeth forth death"* James 1:14-15.

        This shows that we are drawn away by our own _____. *(page 96)*

        What is the end result? _____

    2. Courage is exemplified at times by our ability to _____. *(page 97)*

D. Read about Joseph in Genesis 49–50.

E. Truth is not an _____ in life. It is an _____. Truth will always _____. *(page 98)*

    1. Truth was crucified, laid in a grave and _____. *(page 98)*

    2. Why is it easier for people to believe a lie rather than the truth? *(page 98)*

        _____

    3. People were prejudiced against Joseph because of his _____. *(page 99)*

    4. Assuming you know, instead of asking for the truth, is an example of the sin of _____. *(page 100)*

For Further Study

Impure actions, consequence of impure thoughts – *"A good man out of the good treasure of the heart bringeth forth good things: and an evil man out of the evil treasure bringeth forth evil things"* Matthew 12:35; *"But every man is tempted, when he is drawn away of his own lust, and enticed. Then when lust hath conceived, it bringeth forth sin"* James 1:14-15.

The sin of omission prohibits the character of Christlikeness – *"Lay apart all filthiness and superfluity of naughtiness, and receive with meekness the engrafted word"* James 1:21.

Satan is a spoiler – *"Ye are of your father the devil, and the lusts of your father ye will do. He was a murderer from the beginning"* John 8:44; *"The thief cometh not, but for to steal, and to kill, and to destroy"* John 10:10; Luke 22:31; He wants the place of God – *"How are thou fallen from heaven, O Lucifer, son of the morning … For thou hast said in thine heart, I will ascend into heaven, I will exalt my throne above the stars of God … I will ascend above the heights of the clouds; I will be like the most High"* Isaiah 14:12-15.

F.   What was the determining factor in Joseph's battle? *(page 100)* _____

_____

Match the following: *(pages 100-101)*

____ 1. Joseph fought when he was all   a. truth

____ 2. Who Joseph identified with   b. the honor of God

____ 3. What Joseph was concerned about   c. himself

____ 4. What Joseph's vindication was   d. alone

____ 5. What Joseph was not concerned about   e. God

G.   It is no sin to be _____. *(page 101)*

1.   When you see something that brings up sinful thoughts, you: *(choose one) (page 102)*

____ cannot start praying because you've been tainted with sin.

____ should pray immediately and confess your righteousness in Christ.

2.   If we don't give in to a temptation and Satan accuses us of sin anyway, he's: *(page 102)*

____ Right   ____ Wrong

3.   Since Eve, Satan has always tried to tempt us to sin by giving us: *(circle one) (page 102)*

a. money   b. a half-truth   c. food

4.   What are some meanings of "thinking evil in your hearts"? *(pages 102-103)* _____

_____

5.   Satan has no leverage when there is no: *(circle one) (page 103)*

a. sin   b. women   c. temptation

For Further Study

Courage is sometimes expressed in a decision to flee – Genesis 39:12; 1 Corinthians 6:18; 2 Timothy 2:22.
Satan's first weapon is temptation – *"And immediately the Spirit driveth him into the wilderness. And he was there in the wilderness forty days, tempted of Satan"* Mark 1:12-13; *"For we wrestle not against flesh and blood, but against principalities, against powers, against the rulers of the of the darkness of this world, against spiritual wickedness in high places"* Ephesians 6:12; James 4:7; 1 Peter 5:8-9.
It is not a sin to be tempted – *"And Jesus being full of the Holy Ghost returned from Jordan, and was led by the Spirit into wilderness, Being forty days tempted of the devil"* Luke 4:1-2.
The true test is what we do with the temptation and its author – Proverbs 1:10; *"Submit yourselves therefore to God. Resist the devil, and he will flee from you"* James 4:7; Matthew 26:41; Romans 6:12-13.

6.   The thought is the father to the _____. *(page 103)*

Practical:

1.   Potiphar's wife, with the "spirit of the spoiler," tried to seduce Joseph daily, to bring him down into her sin. How can you recognize the "spirit of the spoiler" when someone tries to take you into sin?

_____

2.   Read: *"Run from anything that gives you the evil thoughts that young men often have, but stay close to anything that makes you want to do right"* 2 Timothy 2:22 TLB.
Sometimes it takes courage to stand and fight. Sometimes it takes more courage to run.
Based on the Scripture above, what situations should ALWAYS be run away from?

_____

3.   A man was accused of theft at work. He could not prove his innocence because it was his word against another man's, and they were both fired. What can he expect God to do for him? What should he do?

_____

_____

Repeat this prayer out loud:

Father, in Jesus' Name, I give You glory for strengthening me against temptation. Thank You for showing me when it's wisdom to flee. Forgive me for lingering with temptation instead of resisting immediately. I choose to be a master of my life, not a victim. Help me make what I've learned a lifelong habit. Amen.

For Further Study

Satan's second weapon is accusation – *"For the accuser of our brethren is cast down, which accused them before our God day and night"* Revelations 12:10; Zechariah 3:1-3.
Jesus Christ is the justifier of the brethren – *"And such were some of you: but ye are washed, but ye are sanctified, but ye are justified in the name of the Lord Jesus, and by the Spirit of our God"* 1 Corinthians 6:11; Romans 3:26; 5:1.
Believing a lie rather than truth – *"And this is the condemnation, that light is come into the world, and men loved darkness rather than light"* John 3:19; 2 Thessalonians 2:10.
Truth will always triumph – *"The lip of truth shall be established for ever: but a lying tongue is but for a moment"* Proverbs 12:19; Psalm 100:5.
Truth was Joseph's vindication – Genesis 41:39-40.
The criteria of holiness is the honor of God – *"How then can I do this great wickedness, and sin against God?"* Genesis 39:9.

Self Test *Lesson 7*

1. Joseph developed his character: *(circle one)*

    a. by being with his brothers   b. while he worked for Potiphar   c. when he was all alone

2. What has a great determining influence on "spur-of-the-moment" decision making?

    _____

    _____

3. What is the criteria of holiness? _____

4. Decision always translates into _____.

5. Sin happens: *(circle one)*

    a. when you're drawn away by your lusts   b. when you're tempted   c. when Satan makes you

6. When you conquer temptation one time, it will never bother you again.   ____ True   ____ False

7. Those who are truly courageous never turn and run.   ____ True   ____ False

8. When Joseph faced the temptation of Potiphar's wife, he was: *(circle one)*

    a. strengthened by his friends   b. all alone   c. at church

9. Listed below are examples of the sin of _____.

    not praying   not meditating on God's Word

    making assumptions   not seeking the truth

10. God can't help you if you're cheated because of your race.   ____ True   ____ False

11. When you feel tempted, it is not necessarily sin.   ____ True   ____ False

12. What is the best way to fight tempting thoughts? _____

    _____

Keep this test for your own records.

Lesson 8

Is God Mad at You? &
When the Innocent Suffer

Lesson 8
Is God Mad at You? &
When the Innocent Suffer

I.   Is God Mad at You? (Chapter 11)

    A.   Name two things that can cause depression. *(page 106)*

        _____   _____

      1.   God is our _____. Satan is our _____. *(page 107)*

      2.   What are some common misperceptions or attitudes men have toward God? *(page 107)*

        a.   _____

        b.   _____

        c.   _____

      3.   Read: *"Then I heard a loud voice shouting across the heavens, 'It has happened at last! God's salvation and the power and the rule, and the authority of his Christ are finally here; for the Accuser of our brothers has been thrown down from heaven on to earth—he accused them day and night before our God. They defeated him by the blood of the Lamb, and by their testimony; for they did not love their lives but laid them down for him'"* Revelation 12:10-11 TLB.

        Who is called "the accuser of the brethren"? *(page 107)* _____

For Further Study
Conviction of sin is from God's love – *"My son, despise not thou the chastening of the Lord, not faint when thou art rebuked of him … For whom the Lord loveth he chasteneth, and scourgeth every son whom he receiveth"* Hebrews 12:5-6.
God wants us to forsake sin so He can bring us a greater revelation of Himself and become more intimate with us – *"When we are judged, we are chastened of the Lord, that we should not be condemned with the world"* 1 Corinthians 11:32; Psalm 94:12-13.
Satan is the accuser, not God – Revelations 12:10; Satan accuses God to man and man to God to put distance between them – Zechariah 3:1-3; Job 1:11.
Some feel God is mad, based on circumstances in their lives – *"And Gideon said unto him, Oh my Lord, if the Lord be with us, why then is all this befallen us?"* Judges 6:13.

4. Satan accuses God to men, and men to God, in order to _____

_____. *(page 107)*

5. What can you believe and receive to change your life? *(page 108)* _____

B. Read Romans 8:31. This Scripture proves that God is _____ us and not _____ us. *(page 109)*

1. Name the three levels of the knowledge of God. *(page 109)*

   a. _____

   b. _____

   c. _____

2. Describe the highest level. *(page 109)*

   _____

   _____

   _____

3. It is impossible for Satan to "bless" someone with earthly riches. *(page 111)*

   ____ True   ____ False

For Further Study

Wrong believing about God will keep you from having an intimate relationship with Him – *"Blessed is he, whosoever shall not be offended in me"* Matthew 11:6.

The three levels of knowledge of God:

God is for me – *"When I cry unto thee, then shall mine enemies turn back: this I know; for God is for me"* Psalm 56:9; Romans 8:31.

God is with me – *"Yea, though I walk through the valley of the shadow of death, I will fear no evil: for thou art with me"* Psalm 23:4; Matthew 1:23.

God is in me – *"Which is Christ in you, the hope of glory"* Colossians 1:27; *"For it is God which worketh in you both to will and to do of his good pleasure"* Philippians 2:13.

God indwells me by His Holy Spirit – *"Know ye not that your body is the temple of the Holy Ghost which is in you, which ye have of God, and ye are not your own?"* 1 Corinthians 6:19.

C.   What you believe about _____ has the greatest potential for good or harm in your life. *(page 112)*

    1.   When God convicts us of sin, it's not because He's mad at us. *(page 112)*

        ____ True   ____ False

    2.   Name at least one thing that happens when we confess our sins. *(page 112)*

       _____

II.   When the Innocent Suffer (Chapter 12)

   A.   Name two difficult things for a man to suffer. *(page 116)*

     _____   _____

    1.   "The innocent suffer for the guilty" is a statement that: *(circle one)* *(page 116)*

       a. is a principle of the cross

       b. is completely unfair

       c. could not possibly be right

For Further Study

God is at work at all times to produce our highest good, His perfect will – *"And we know that all things work together for good to them that love God, to them who are the called according to his purpose"* Romans 8:28; Psalm 139; Philippians 2:12-13.

Your belief about God, the greatest potential in life – *"For I am not ashamed of the gospel of Christ: for it is the power of God unto salvation to every one that believeth"* Romans 1:16; *"Because that, when they knew God, they glorified him not as God, neither were thankful; but became vain in their imaginations, and their foolish heart was darkened"* Romans 1:21.

What you believe can attract or repel – Job 3:25; Mark 11:23.

What you believe about God will determine your relationship with Him – *"For he that cometh to God must believe that he is, and that he is a rewarder of them that diligently seek him"* Hebrews 11:6.

2. It is okay to tell God our real feelings about something. *(circle one)* *(page 117)*

   a. never—you should always get over it before you start to pray

   b. only when you're absolutely desperate

   c. anytime—He understands

3. By not forgiving your parents, you can actually retain their sins in your life. *(page 120)*

   ____ True   ____ False

4. Write out Genesis 50:20. Then circle the **two key words** in the Scripture.

   _____

   _____

   _____

B. The Gospel is _____. *(page 123)*

   Men just give _____. *(page 123)*

For Further Study

What you believe about yourself will determine your relationships with others – Proverbs 23:7.

Joseph believed God was a good God, God loved him and God was working on his behalf – Genesis 45:5; 50:20; Psalm 105:17-22.

The innocent suffer for the guilty – *"For I (Joseph) was kidnapped from my homeland among the Hebrews, and now this—here I am in jail when I did nothing to deserve it"* Genesis 40:15 TLB.

It is hard to suffer when you are innocent – *"For what glory is it, if, when ye be buffeted for your faults, ye shall take it patiently? but if, when ye do well, and suffer for it, ye take it patiently, this is acceptable with God"* 1 Peter 2:20; 3:14; Matthew 5:11-12.

Standing for righteousness may bring persecution, ridicule and rejection – *"Yea, and all that will live godly in Christ Jesus shall suffer persecution"* 2 Timothy 3:12; The fire you go through will purify and strengthen you – Jeremiah 15:19, 20; 1 Peter 1:7.

C. Look up and read out loud 1 Timothy 5:22. Write the key phrase from this Scripture that is used in this chapter. _____

_____

1. Being in partnership with a guilty man can cause you to suffer regardless of your innocence. *(page 125)* _____ True _____ False

2. Read: *"Whoever is partner with a thief hates his own life; he falls under the curse [pronounced upon him who knows who the thief is] but discloses nothing"* Proverbs 29:24 AMP.

D. Everything in life has the potential for _____ or _____. *(page 126)*

Practical:

1. Give examples of the three levels of the knowledge of God. *(page 109)*

   Which level are you on?

   _____

For Further Study

Maturation is a lifelong process – *"We also rejoice in our sufferings, because we know that suffering produces perseverance; perseverance, character; and character, hope"* Romans 5:3-5 NIV; Romans 8:37; Galatians 6:9; Hebrews 3:6; 6:1; 1 John 3:2, 3.

Jesus Christ bore all the hurt, bitterness, shame and resentment on the cross – Isaiah 53:4-5; Hebrews 12:2; 1 Peter 2:21-22.

Recognize how God has forgiven you – *"For as the heaven is high above the earth, so great is his mercy toward them that fear him. As far as the east is from the west, so far hath he removed our transgressions from us"* Psalm 103:11-12; Jeremiah 31:34.

Forgive those who have harmed you, so you can release their sins out of your life – *"And when ye stand praying, forgive, if ye have aught against any: that your Father also which is in heaven may forgive you your trespasses"* Mark 11:25; Matthew 5:23-24; John 20:22-23.

2. Do you ever feel like God is mad at you? In your opinion, why is it hard to believe God is a good God Who is always working toward our highest good? _____

_____

_____

3. George was thinking about guaranteeing a car loan so a friend who worked only sporadically could get a full-time job. Is he being willing to "suffer for the guilty"? Or is he "partaking in another man's sins"? In your opinion, what factors does he need to consider?

_____

_____

Repeat this prayer out loud:

Father, in Jesus' Name, forgive me for accusing others, for being in agreement with "the accuser of the brethren," instead of being in agreement with You. Forgive me also for entertaining accusations against You, for believing that You are anything other than the good God You truly are. And when I suffer unjustly, please help me bring glory to You by humbling myself to Your Word and remembering the cross. I give my life to You, for You to be glorified in my life, regardless of circumstances. Amen.

For Further Study

Do not partake in another man's sins – *"Lay hands suddenly on no man, neither be partaker of other men's sins: keep thyself pure"* 1 Timothy 5:22; *"Whoso is partner with a thief hateth his own soul: he heareth cursing, and betrayeth it not"* Proverbs 29:24.

Realize the situation has potential for good as well as harm – Romans 8:28.

Submit the circumstances to God instead of rebelling against them – *"[Jesus] Who, when he was reviled, reviled not again; when he suffered, he threatened not; but committed himself to him that judgeth righteously"* 1 Peter 2:23; *"Humble yourselves therefore under the mighty hand of God, that he may exalt you in due time: Casting all your care upon him; for he careth for you"* 1 Peter 5:6-7.

Self Test *Lesson 8*

1. Satan is called the _____.

2. **In your own words,** name some situations that may cause men to resent God.

   a. _____

   b. _____

   c. _____

3. Name the three levels of the knowledge of God.

   a. _____

   b. _____

   c. _____

4. It doesn't matter what you believe about God because He's going to do what He wants anyway.

   _____ True   _____ False

5. What you believe about God holds the greatest potential for good or harm in life.

   _____ True   _____ False

6. When God convicts us of sin, it is an expression of His anger toward us.   _____ True   _____ False

7. It's not scriptural for the innocent to suffer for the guilty.   _____ True   _____ False

8. By not forgiving your parents, you can actually retain their sins in your life.   _____ True   _____ False

9. In 1 Timothy 5:22, we learn that we are not to be _____.

10. The Gospel is: *(circle one)*

    a. good news   b. good advice   c. a good idea

Keep this test for your own records.

Lesson 9

Set a Priority or Two

Lesson 9
Set a Priority or Two

A. Pressure always _____. *(page 127)*

   1. The difference in men who _____ and _____ is in their ability to handle

   _____. *(page 128)*

   2. Pressure is a modern phenomenon, not experienced by previous generations. *(pages 128-129)*

   ____ True   ____ False

   3. What did Jesus do with pressure? *(circle all that apply)* *(page 129)*

   a. faced it   c. overcame it   e. rose triumphant over it

   b. ran from it   d. avoided it   f. cursed it

B. Men who become heroes and accomplish great things are men who have a _____

   _____ in which their priorities are set correctly. *(page 129)*

C. Some things in life are _____. *(page 130)*

   1. Write out Acts 20:24. _____

   _____

   _____

   _____

For Further Study

Pressure always magnifies – *"Saying, Father, if thou be willing, remove this cup from me: nevertheless not my will, but thine be done. ... And being in an agony he prayed more earnestly: and his sweat was as great drops of blood falling down to the ground"* Luke 22:42-44.

The difference between men who succeed and men who fail is in their ability to handle pressure – *"But a certain maid beheld him as he sat by the fire, and earnestly looked upon him, and said, This man was also with him. And he denied him, saying, Woman, I know him not"* Luke 22:54-57; *"And David was greatly distressed; for the people spake of stoning him, because the soul of all the people was grieved, every man for his sons and for his daughters: but David encouraged himself in the Lord his God"* 1 Samuel 30:6.

2.   Name some Bible characters who considered something of Godly value as more important than their own lives. *(page 130)*

_____

3.   Name some Bible characters who considered something foolish as more important than God and

their lives. *(pages 130-131)* _____

D.   Read Genesis 25:27-34.
Some men are willing to trade their birthright, God's destiny for their lives, for something of lesser value. Their value system is out of priority. Give a reason why men do that. *(page 130)*

_____

E.   Read 1 Samuel 2:12-17 and 3:11-13.

Why was Eli's posterity cut off? *(page 131)*

_____

F.   Read Mark 5:21-43.

What are some of the things Jairus laid aside for his daughter's healing? *(page 131)*

_____

For Further Study

Jesus faced the ultimate pressure and overcame it; whoever believes in Him and receives His Spirit can live in the same way – *"Looking unto Jesus the author and finisher of our faith; who for the joy that was set before him endured the cross, despising the shame, and is set down at the right hand of the throne of God. For consider him that endured such contradiction of sinners against himself, lest ye be wearied and faint in your minds"* Hebrews 12:2-3; Philippians 2:8-9.

Some things in life are more important than life itself – *"Even as the Son of man came ... to give his life a ransom for many"* Matthew 20:28; Matthew 10:39.

Discipline is the correct application of pressure – 1 Corinthians 9:27.

One of the tests of manhood is how a man handles pressure – Proverbs 24:10.

Men must be tested and proven before they can be given authority – James 1:12.

G. Look at the pairs of phrases below and circle the one from each pair that is most important: *(pages 131, 134)*

the will of God   **or**   your children

ministering God's healing   **or**   your personal faith in God

your position, power, prestige, pride   **or**   your daughter's healing

Practical:

1. Have you experienced a time when pressure magnified a situation? If yes, when?

_____

_____

2. Read out loud Philippians 3:8. Read again Acts 20:24.

How do your priorities differ from Paul's? *(not necessary to write down)*

For Further Study

Courage: It takes courage to resist peer pressure and dare to be different – Psalm 119:51, 52; Daniel 1:8. It takes courage to submit to righteousness – Psalm 119:30. It takes courage to say "no" – *"I have refrained my feet from every evil way, that I might keep thy word"* Psalm 119:101; It takes courage to admit a desire to be a man of God – *"Depart from me, ye evildoers: for I will keep the commandments of my God"* Psalm 119:115; *"Choosing rather to suffer affliction with the people of God, than to enjoy the pleasures of sin for a season"* Hebrews 11:25. Men who become heroes must also have a value system in which their priorities are set aright – *"But seek ye first the kingdom of God, and his righteousness; and all these things shall be added unto you"* Matthew 6:33; Daniel 6:7-10.

3. Determine what has been more important to you than the Lord by repeating out loud the sentence below, filling in the blank with each phrase listed, one by one. After determining, mark "True" or "False" after each. "It's more important to me that I _____ than obey God and defend the honor of God."

		True		False
a.	make money	____ True	____ False	
b.	sleep in	____ True	____ False	
c.	try to make my wife happy	____ True	____ False	
d.	do things for my children	____ True	____ False	
e.	buy things	____ True	____ False	
f.	fix up my car	____ True	____ False	
g.	leave the church	____ True	____ False	
h.	stay at the same church	____ True	____ False	
i.	watch or play sports	____ True	____ False	
j.	keep my hobbies	____ True	____ False	
k.	build a career	____ True	____ False	
l.	maintain my own pride	____ True	____ False	
m.	keep others from thinking I'm a "fanatic"	____ True	____ False	
n.	stay busy ministering to everyone	____ True	____ False	
o.	continue my "secret sin"	____ True	____ False	

Repeat this prayer out loud:

Father, in Jesus' Name, it's hard to see myself as I really am. I'm not as much of a man as I thought I was. Please forgive me. I'm sorry for counting my life dear and not giving my all to You to fight for the victories I need in my life, my family, my church and the world around me. I refuse to give up my birthright in Christ anymore for a moment's pleasure or for personal desires. I resist the pressure to give in with the overcoming power of Jesus Christ that You've placed within me. I surrender my life to You once again today, that You might be glorified in me. Thank You, Father, for loving me even in my sin. Amen.

For Further Study

Men to whom God is most important – *"But none of these things move me, neither count I my life dear unto myself, so that I might finish my course with joy, and the ministry, which I have received of the Lord Jesus, to testify the gospel of the grace of God"* Acts 20:24; John the Baptist, executed for refusing to compromise – Matthew 14:3-11; Stephen, stoned for his stand for righteousness – Acts 7:54-60; Jesus Christ, gave His life for our salvation – John 10:17-18.

Men for whom God was less important – Esau sold his birthright for a mess of pottage – Genesis 25:29-34; Eli indulged his sons at the expense of the Word of God – 1 Samuel 2; 3.

We give all for our Lord – *"Yea doubtless, and I count all things but loss for the excellency of the knowledge of Christ Jesus my Lord: for whom I have suffered the loss of all things, and do count them but dung, that I may win Christ"* Philippians 3:8.

Self Test *Lesson 9*

1. Pressure always _____.

2. The difference between men who succeed or men who fail is their ability to handle _____.

3. Jesus knew the ultimate pressure. How did He deal with it?

   a. _____

   b. _____

   c. _____

4. Men who become heroes and accomplish great things are not only men who know how to handle pressure, but men who also have what? _____

   _____.

5. Some things in life are _____.

6. What did Esau lose because of his fleshly desire? _____

7. Why did Eli ultimately lose his life and ministry?

   _____

8. Jairus was a ruler of the synagogue. What did he lay aside in order to see his need met?

   _____

Keep this test for your own records.

Lesson 10
Are You Ready to Prosper?

Lesson 10
Are You Ready to Prosper?

A. Read Genesis 39:2.

Was Joseph a prosperous man? *(page 135)* ___ Yes ___ No

B. Name the three basic problem areas in relationships. *(page 135)*

1. _____ 2. _____ 3. _____

C. The use of money is a _____ of faith. *(page 135)*

1. What a man does with his _____ shows what a man does with his life and how much

_____ he places in it. *(page 135)*

2. Money is the closest thing to _____ most men will ever have. *(page 135)*

3. Name some things money cannot buy. *(page 136)*

a. _____

b. _____

c. _____

For Further Study

What you believe about money will attract or repel it – Genesis 39:2; Proverbs 11:24, 28.

Money is amoral. We give it morality or immorality – *"And I say unto you, Make to yourselves friends of the mammon of unrighteousness; that, when ye fail, they may receive you into everlasting habitations"* Luke 16:9; *"Charge them that are rich in this world, that they be not high-minded, nor trust in uncertain riches, but in the living God, who giveth us richly all things to enjoy"* 1 Timothy 6:17.

Money has the potential for blessing or cursing. Money is a means, not an end – *"He that hath a bountiful eye shall be blessed; for he giveth of his bread to the poor"* Proverbs 22:9; *"No man can serve two masters: for either he will hate the one, and love the other; or else he will hold to the one, and despise the other. Ye cannot serve God and mammon"* Matthew 6:24.

D. Write in the letter of the word that completes the following statements: *(pages 136-137)*

___ 1. What you believe will attract or   a. love

___ 2. The image you have of money determines your   b. tithing

___ 3. Money is   c. pride

___ 4. Money is not all there is to   d. covetousness

___ 5. Tithing is not all there is to   e. repel

___ 6. Stewardship includes time, talent and   f. amoral

___ 7. A man won't tithe because of unbelief, fear or   g. spirit

___ 8. Ministers don't preach on money due to unbelief, fear or   h. stewardship

___ 9. Giving is a release to the   i. beliefs

___ 10. Giving is an expression of   j. treasure

For Further Study

The root of all evil – *"For the (covetous, avaricious) love of money is the root of all evil: which while some coveted after, they have erred from the faith, and pierced themselves through with many sorrows"* 1 Timothy 6:10.

Tithing is not all there is to stewardship – *"And this they did, not as we hoped, but first gave their own selves to the Lord, and unto us by the will of God"* 2 Corinthians 8:1-3, 5.

Tithing time, talent and treasury – 1 Corinthians 6:19-20

Three reasons why men won't tithe money:

Unbelief – *"Bring ye all the tithes into the storehouse ... and prove me now ... if I will not open you the windows of heaven, and pour you out a blessing"* Malachi 3:10.

Fear – *"And I will rebuke the devourer for your sakes"* Malachi 3:11.

Covetousness – *"Will a man rob God? Yet ye have robbed me ... In tithes and offerings"* Malachi 3:8.

E.   You know the depth of loving only by the degree of _____. *(page 137)*

1.   Offerings in the church are not for the health of the _____ but for the

health of the _____. *(page 137)*

2.   Write out Deuteronomy 8:18.

_____

_____

_____

3.   Why does God want His people to prosper financially? *(pages 137-138)*

_____

4.   The purpose for money is _____, not _____. *(page 138)*

F.   Write out 1 Timothy 6:10. _____

_____

_____

1.   Money is the root of all evil. *(page 138)*   ___ True   ___ False

For Further Study

Giving is a release to the spirit – Isaiah 58:6-8.

Giving is an expression of love – 2 Corinthians 8:1-4.

You know the depth of love by the degree of giving – *"For God so loved the world, that he gave his only begotten Son, that whosoever believeth in him should not perish, but have everlasting life"* John 3:16; *"Greater love hath no man than this, that a man lay down his life for his friends"* John 15:13.

Offerings are not for the health of the preacher but for the health of the congregation – *"Honour the Lord with thy substance, and with the firstfruits of all thine increase: So shall thy barns be filled with plenty, and thy presses shall burst out with new wine"* Proverbs 3:9-10; *"But thou shalt remember the Lord thy God: for it is he that giveth thee power to get wealth, that he may establish his covenant which he sware unto thy fathers, as it is this day"* Deuteronomy 8:18.

2. Obedience is the evidence of _____. *(page 138)*

3. A ton of prayer will never _____.
   (page 138)

4. Read 1 Samuel 15:22. Write the key phrase. *(page 138)*

   _____

5. We cannot compensate by _____ what we lose through

   _____. *(page 139)*

G. Why are an altar call and an offering synonymous? *(page 140)*

   _____

1. Poverty and spirituality are synonymous. *(page 141)*   ___ True ___ False

2. Read Mark 10:24. Why did Jesus say it would be difficult for some who are rich to enter into the

   Kingdom of God? _____

For Further Study

God prospers His people so more can be given to the work of the Lord – *"Yes, God will give you much so that you can give away much, and when we take your gifts to those who need them they will break out into thanksgiving and praise to God for your help"* 2 Corinthians 9:8, 10, 11 TLB.

You cannot compensate by sacrifice what you lose through disobedience – *"Behold, to obey is better than sacrifice, and to hearken than the fat of rams"* 1 Samuel 15:22.

If we love Jesus, we'll obey Him – *"If ye love me, keep my commandments"* John 14:15.

Obedience is the evidence of love – *"He that hath my commandments, and keepeth them, he it is that loveth me"* John 14:21.

Manifestation is based on obedience – *"And he that loveth me shall be loved of my Father, and I will love him, and will manifest myself to him … If a man love me, he will keep my words: and my Father will love him, and we will come unto him, and make our abode with him"* John 14:21, 23.

3. Poverty is a _____. *(page 141)*

4. The principle of the Kingdom is that you give to: *(page 142)*

   a. get rid of it   b. lose   c. gain

5. All money has is: *(page 143)*

   a. evil   b. potential   c. trouble

H. Define prostitution. *(page 144)* _____

1. Loving God only for material prosperity is _____. *(page 144)*

2. It is the nature of God to _____. *(page 144)*

3. To deny through unbelief God's right to prosper you materially is to deny _____

   _____. *(page 145)*

For Further Study

Prayer will not bring God's financial blessings if you are disobeying God by not tithing – *"If I regard iniquity in my heart, the Lord will not hear me"* Psalm 66:18.

You give your life to Jesus at the altar – Matthew 10:39; You place your life in the offering plate – *"For this (is) proof that your deeds are as good as your doctrine"* 2 Corinthians 9:13 TLB.

The issue isn't being rich or poor but being obedient – *"Jesus answereth … Children, how hard is it for them that trust in riches to enter into the kingdom of God!"* Mark 10:24.

That which is visible is made up of that which is invisible – Hebrews 11:3; Love is invisible; giving is visible – *"For God so loved the world, that he gave his only begotten Son, that whosoever believeth in him should not perish, but have everlasting life"* John 3:16; Honor is invisible; obedience is visible – Luke 6:46; The degree of invisible love is evidenced by the degree of visible giving – *"Hereby perceive we the love of God, because he laid down his life for us: and we ought to lay down our lives for the brethren"* 1 John 3:16.

Practical:

1. "You cannot compensate by sacrifice what you lose through disobedience." What does that mean?

   _____

   _____

2. Read Proverbs 14:23; 24:30-34; Luke 6:38. Name two reasons some men struggle with money.

   _____

   _____

Repeat this prayer out loud:

Lord God, I repent of my attitudes about money and ask You to help me believe Your Word about money, both the lack of it and the abundance of it. I accept, by faith, Your prosperity now, in Jesus' Name. Amen.

For Further Study

The quality of love for God is reflected in obedience – John 14:21; Giving cannot be a substitute for obedience – 1 Samuel 15:22; Proverbs 21:27.

We cannot outgive God – *"Give, and it shall be given unto you; good measure, pressed down, and shaken together, and running over, shall men give into your bosom"* Luke 6:38.

Financial health based on faith – *"He which soweth sparingly shall reap also sparingly; and he which soweth bountifully shall reap also bountifully"* 2 Corinthians 9:6; *"Honour the Lord with thy substance, and with the firstfruits of all thine increase: So shall thy barns be filled with plenty, and thy presses shall burst out with new wine"* Proverbs 3:9-10; James 2:17-20.

Jesus cared how people used money – Matthew 19:21; Mark 12:41; Luke 19:8; Acts 5:1-2.

Covetous v. Generous – *"It is possible to give away and become richer! It is also possible to hold on too tightly and lose everything. Yes, the liberal man shall be rich! By watering others, he waters himself"* Proverbs 11:24-25 TLB; *"He that is greedy of gain troubleth his own house"* Proverbs 15:27; 28:27; Colossians 3:5.

Self Test *Lesson 10*

1. The use of money is a visible expression of _____.

2. What you believe about money will either attract it or repel it. ____ True ____ False

3. The only morality money has is the morality we give it through our use of it. ____ True ____ False

4. Name the three areas of your life from which you should be tithing.

   a. _____ b. _____ c. _____

5. Name three reasons men won't tithe their money.

   a. _____

   b. _____

   c. _____

6. Offerings in church are to help the preacher. ____ True ____ False

7. God's purpose in prospering His people is for them to stockpile money. ____ True ____ False

8. Which is correct? *(check one)*

   ____ Money is the root of all evil.

   ____ The love of money is the root of all evil.

9. Obedience is the evidence of _____.

10. We cannot _____ by sacrifice what we lose through _____.

11. Why can it be said that an offering and an altar call are synonymous?

   _____

12. What is "spiritual prostitution"?

   _____

Keep this test for your own records.

Lesson 11
Guilt? Who Needs It!

Lesson 11
Guilt? Who Needs It!

A. Name the three immediate results of sin. *(page 148)*

1. _____   2. _____   3. _____

Guilt produces _____ which produces _____. *(page 148)*

B. You cannot get the guilt out of your life until you: *(page 149)*

_____

1. Once God has forgiven you, then you need to _____. *(page 149)*

2. When we forgive, we don't necessarily _____. *(page 149)*

For Further Study

The results of sin – Guilt, Fear and Hiding – *"And the Lord God called unto Adam, and said unto him, Where art thou? And he said, I heard thy voice in the garden, and I was afraid, because I was naked; and I hid myself"* Genesis 3:9-10.

You cannot get the guilt out of your life until you ask God to forgive you – *"There was a time when I wouldn't admit what a sinner I was. But my dishonesty made me miserable and filled my days with frustration … until I finally admitted all my sins to you and stopped trying to hide them. I said to myself, 'I will confess them to the Lord.' And you forgave me! All my guilt is gone"* Psalm 32:3-5 TLB.

When we confess our sins, God forgives us and no longer holds them against us – *"If we confess our sins, he is faithful and just to forgive us our sins, and to cleanse us from all unrighteousness"* 1 John 1:9.

3. Name some things you will no longer have to retain once you have completely forgiven and received forgiveness. *(pages 149-150)*

    _____

    _____

4. How did Joseph feel about his brothers who had sold him? *(page 150)*

    _____

    _____

5. Joseph's experiences weren't good, but ultimately they worked out good. *(page 150)*

    _____ True   _____ False

6. Guilt is _____. It kills _____. *(page 151)*

For Further Study

By the help of God, through the presence of His Holy Spirit, you can forgive others as God forgives you –
"Receive ye the Holy Ghost: Whosoever sins ye remit, they are remitted unto them; and whosoever sins ye retain, they are retained" John 20:22-23.
Because they had never asked for and received forgiveness, Joseph's brothers could not release their guilt – *"When Joseph's brethren saw that their father was dead, they said, Joseph will peradventure hate us, and will certainly requite us all the evil which we did unto him"* Genesis 50:15.
The principal of release states that only after sins are released are people free to become what God wants them to be – Matthew 6:14, 15.

C. Read Romans 7:24-25.

    1. Describe the custom Paul referred to from those days. *(page 152)*

    _____

    _____

    _____

    _____

    2. Paul was referring to the burden of _____ from our sins. *(page 153)*

    3. What is Paul's great statement of truth? *(page 153)*

    _____

    We're free from the guilt and sin of the past.

    4. When Jesus Christ forgives us of our sins, they are _____ from us, never to be

    _____ against us again. *(page 153)*

For Further Study

The sins you forgive are released, and the sins you do not forgive are retained in your life – "*[Now having received the Holy Spirit, and being led and directed by Him] if you forgive the sins of anyone, they are forgiven; if you retain the sins of anyone, they are retained*" John 20:23 AMP.

Healing takes place when, by faith, the principle of release is acted upon – Hebrews 12:1.

In order to activate this principle in your life, admit the Holy Spirit into your heart and be guided and directed by Him – "*Then Jesus … breathed on them and said to them, Receive (admit) the Holy Spirit!*" John 20:21, 22 AMP.

5. Read: *"I, even I, am he that blotteth out thy transgressions for mine own sake, and will not remember thy sins"* Isaiah 43:25.

6. Read: *"He has removed our sins as far away from us as the east is from the west"* Psalm 103:12 TLB.

7. You can be free from guilt, but you'll never be free from the past. *(page 153)*

    _____ True   _____ False

D. If God forgives us of our sins and we do not forgive ourselves, then we make ourselves _____

   _____. *(page 153)*

For Further Study

When Jesus Christ forgives our sins, they are severed from us – *"O wretched man that I am! who shall deliver me from the body of this death? I thank God through Jesus Christ our Lord. So then with the mind I myself serve the law of God; but with the flesh the law of sin"* Romans 7:24-25; *"As far as the east is from the west, so far hath he removed our transgressions from us"* Psalm 103:12.

You are light-hearted when you are not burdened with guilt – Psalm 32:5.

Guilt is a killer – Psalm 32:3-5.

God forgives, then forgets, our sins – Psalms 32:1, 2; 85:2; 103:12; Isaiah 43:25; Romans 4:7, 8.

1. "We can be free from and also free to ..." *(page 154)*

   Following the example, write down some things we're "free from" and "free to."

   FREE FROM   **FREE TO**

   Hatred _____   Love _____

   _____   _____

   _____   _____

   _____   _____

   _____   _____

   _____   _____

2. Releasing our guilt produces _____. *(page 154)*

Practical:

1. Ask God to clearly define and reveal to you areas of guilt which you may have covered over the years.

   Are your decisions today still affected by the pains of past events? _____

For Further Study

We are forgiven – Psalm 103:8-13; Micah 7:18, 19; *"Blessed is he whose transgressions are forgiven, whose sins are covered"* Psalm 32:1-7 NIV; *"I, even I, am he that blotteth out thy transgressions for mine own sake, and will not remember thy sins"* Isaiah 43:25.

If God forgives us and we do not forgive ourselves, then we make ourselves greater than God – *"Who shall lay any thing to the charge of God's elect? It is God that justifieth. Who is he that condemneth? It is Christ that died, yea rather, that is risen again, who is even at the right hand of God, who also maketh intercession for us"* Romans 8:33-34.

There is joy in releasing our guilt to Jesus – *"Purge me with hyssop, and I shall be clean: wash me, and I shall be whiter than snow ... Restore unto me the joy of thy salvation; and uphold me with thy free spirit"* Psalm 51:7, 12.

2.   Search your heart and be sure you have forgiven yourself for every sin.

3.   Write out Ephesians 4:32.

_____

_____

_____

How important is it to forgive others? To forgive yourself?

_____

4.   Write out John 8:36.

_____

Write **in your own words** what that verse means to you.

_____

_____

Repeat this prayer out loud:

Father, in Jesus' Name, I refuse to carry the weight of death and guilt with me anymore. Forgive me for letting it hinder me and Your work in me. I forgive everyone for everything—sins against me, money they owe me—and I sow it into Your Kingdom for You to turn what was meant for evil into good. And I forgive myself. I choose to walk in the freedom Christ's blood provided for me at Calvary. I am free! Free to worship You, free to excel, free to bless and to be blessed. Thank You for truth that sets me free. Amen.

For Further Study

Forgiven means free from guilt – *"Let us draw near with a true heart in full assurance of faith, having our hearts sprinkled from an evil conscience"* Hebrews 10:22.

Forgiven means free to love – *"Love (God's love in us) does not insist on its own rights or its own way, for it is not self-seeking; it is not touchy or fretful or resentful; it take no account of the evil done to it [it pays no attention to a suffered wrong]"* 1 Corinthians 13:5 AMP.

Forgiven means free to worship and serve God – *"How much more shall the blood of Christ, who through the eternal Spirit offered himself without spot to God, purge your conscience from dead works to serve the living God?"* Hebrews 9:14.

Self Test *Lesson 11*

1. Name the immediate results of sin.

   a. _____

   b. _____

   c. _____

2. What is the cure for guilt? *(circle one)*

   a. prayer　　　b. fasting　　　c. forgiveness

3. Once God has forgiven you, you must forgive _____.

4. The way you'll know that you really forgave is that you completely forget.　____ True　____ False

5. What effect can guilt have on relationships? _____

6. What was Paul referring to when he asked, *"Who shall deliver me from this body of death?"* Romans 7:24 AMP?

   _____

7. Holding on to a little guilt can be a good thing, as it will keep us humble.　____ True　____ False

8. If we do not forgive ourselves of our sins, what have we done in relationship to God?

   _____

Keep this test for your own records.

Lesson 12

The Price of Peace &
Principles for Success

Lesson 12

The Price of Peace &
Principles for Success

I. The Price of Peace (Chapter 16)

    A. To love someone is to _____. *(page 155)*

        1. Joseph's love for his brothers held the potential for their _____. *(page 155)*

        2. The command to repent is actually an act of love. *(page 155)*   ____ True   ____ False

        3. Being nice is not always being _____. *(page 156)*

    B. Write out Matthew 5:13.

    _____

    _____

    _____

For Further Study

Conviction of sin and chastening are manifestations of love – *"My son, despise not the chastening of the Lord; neither be weary of his correction: For whom the Lord loveth he correcteth; even as a father the son in whom he delighteth"* Proverbs 3:11-12.

Sin left in our lives prevents God's intimacy with us – *"Draw nigh to God, and he will draw nigh to you. Cleanse you hands, ye sinners; and purify your hearts, ye double-minded"* James 4:7-8; *"Ye are the salt of the earth: but if the salt have lost his savour, wherewith shall it be salted? it is thenceforth good for nothing, but to be cast out, and to be trodden under foot of men"* Matthew 5:13; *"And unto the married I command, yet not I, but the Lord, Let not the wife depart from her husband"* 1 Corinthians 7:10.

Crisis is normal to life – *"In the world ye shall have tribulation"* John 16:33.

C.   When a man feels guilty because his wife commits adultery, he needs to: *(page 159)*

1.   Face the _____.

2.   Reject her _____.

3.   _____ her sin.

4.   _____ yours.

5.   Ask God for _____.

6.   When God forgives you, _____.

7.   Renew your relationship with _____.

8.   Get your life in line with the _____ and get on with it!

D.   _____ and _____ are not repentance. *(page 159)*

1.   Write out 1 Corinthians 7:10. _____
     _____

2.   Sorrow has the potential for being one of life's greatest teachers. *(page 160)*

     _____ True   _____ False

For Further Study

Crisis has sorrow in it, but sorrow is life's greatest teacher – Ecclesiastes 7:3; *"It is good for me that I have been afflicted; that I might learn thy statutes"* Psalm 119:71.

All true joy is born out of sorrow – *"Weeping may endure for a night, but joy cometh in the morning"* Psalm 30:5; *"They that sow in tears shall reap in joy"* Psalm 126:5.

God wants every change in the lives of His children to be good – Romans 8:28.

Joy is birthed out of sorrow – *"Ye shall be sorrowful, but your sorrow shall be turned into joy. A woman when she is in travail hath sorrow, because her hour is come: but as soon as she is delivered of the child, she remembereth no more the anguish, for joy that a man is born into the world"* John 16:20-21; Esther 9:22; Psalms 30:11; 126:5, 6; Jeremiah 31:9-17.

3. Using the words below, fill in the following sentences: *(page 160)*

    sorrow   repentance   reconciliation   fellowship

    Without _____ for sin, there is no _____.

    Without _____ there is no _____.

    Without _____ there is no _____ with God.

4. Read Hebrews 12:5-8.

    Why does God chasten us? _____ *(page 160)*

5. Conviction of sin in our life is not an evidence of God's _____ but of

    His _____. *(page 160)*

E. Peace and _____ are not synonymous. *(page 161)*

    1. We should try to achieve peace at any price. *(page 161)*   ___ True   ___ False

    2. Read Ephesians 4:15. Truth must be spoken in _____. *(page 161)*

For Further Study

Without sorrow for sin, there cannot be repentance – *"Now I rejoice, not that ye were made sorry, but that ye sorrowed to repentance: for ye were made sorry after a godly manner ... For godly sorrow worketh repentance to salvation not to be repented of"* 2 Corinthians 7:9-10.

Without repentance, there cannot be reconciliation and fellowship with God – *"Let the wicked forsake his way, and the unrighteous man his thoughts: and let him return unto the Lord, and he will have mercy upon him; and to our God, for he will abundantly pardon"* Isaiah 55:7.

Peace and passivity are not the same – *"Peace I leave with you, my peace I give unto you: not as the world giveth, give I unto you"* John 14:27.

We are to love our enemies but not capitulate to them – *"Be not overcome of evil, but overcome evil with good"* Romans 12:19-21.

F.   Match the following: *(pages 161-163)*

   ___ 1. The supreme goal of people   a. openness

   ___ 2. God's desire above all things   b. vulnerability

   ___ 3. A "must" to achieve intimacy   c. intimate relationship with you

   ___ 4. You cannot have openness without   d. religion

   ___ 5. You cannot get intimacy with God with e. defenses

   ___ 6. Christianity is a loving   f. intimacy in a relationship

   ___ 7. Intimacy depends on dropping   g. relationship with a living God

G.   Write out Luke 9:24.

_____

_____

For Further Study

Peace at any price is devilish, not divine – *"Think not that I am come to send peace on earth: I came not to send peace, but a sword"* Matthew 10:34.

Truth must always be spoken in love – *"But speaking the truth in love, may grow up into him in all things"* Ephesians 4:15.

The pattern of the parable of the prodigal:

Rebellion: Sin never cares about anything except gratifying its own desires – Luke 15:12.

Ruin: The prodigal began his ruin with the words, "Give me" – Luke 15:13, 14.

Repentance: The pivotal point between ruin and reconciliation is characterized by the words, "Make me" – Luke 15:17, 19.

Reconciliation: The prodigal returns home to his father – Luke 15:20.

Restoration: The father accepts the son and restores him to his rightful position – Luke 15:22-24.

II. Principles for Success (Epilogue)

    A. Name some things Joseph overcame in life. *(page 165)*_____

_____

        1. What was more important, Joseph's ability to submit or to resist? *(page 165)*

            _____

        2. Describe God's transcendent glory. *(pages 165-166)*_____

            _____

            _____

    B. Place a "T" or "F" next to statements that are "True" or "False." *(pages 166-168)*

      ___ Every Christian is to live a crucified life.

      ___ God has no plan for failure for those who are submitted to Him.

      ___ Everything in life has potential.

      ___ What you believe has nothing to do with what actually happens.

      ___ Success comes by working through our strengths, not dwelling on our weaknesses.

      ___ Words have creative power.

      ___ The image we have of God will have no effect on our lives.

      ___ The image we have of ourselves contributes to our self-confidence.

      ___ Satan's weapons are temptation and accusation.

      ___ Sorrow has no place in a Christian's life.

For Further Study

God chastens us – Hebrews 12:5-8.

Christ is the head – Ephesians 4:15.

We lose our life by finding it in identification with Jesus Christ – *"For whosoever will save his life shall lose it: but whosoever will lose his life for my sake, the same shall save it"* Luke 9:24-25; *"It is a faithful saying: For if we be dead with him, we shall also live with him: If we suffer, we shall also reign with him: if we deny him, he also will deny us"* 2 Timothy 2:11-12; Matthew 10:32-33; 12:30.

Joseph was certain in his identification with God – *"Now therefore be not grieved, nor angry with yourselves, that ye sold me hither: for God did send me before you to preserve life"* Genesis 45:5; and knew God had spoken to him – *"But as for you, ye thought evil against me; but God meant it unto good, to bring to pass, as it is this day, to save much people alive"* Genesis 50:20.

Practical:

1.   In the illustration about a man whose wife committed adultery, should he have tried to win her back?

     What circumstances would change your mind, and what would he need to do? *(page 124)*

     _____

     _____

2.   Read John 4:1-30. What did the woman have to do to become friends with Jesus?

     _____

Repeat this prayer out loud:

Father, in Jesus' Name, help me to understand the kind of intimacy You want with me and what stands in my way. I repent of barriers that keep me from You, both those I know and those I'm not even aware of. Thank You for Your love for me that is so hard to understand. I love You, Lord. Amen.

For Further Study

Joseph's faith outlasted his life – *"By faith Joseph, when he died, made mention of the departing of the children of Israel; and gave commandment concerning his bones"* Hebrews 11:22.

Crucify the flesh, but live a resurrected life – *"For if we have been planted together in the likeness of his death, we shall be also in the likeness of his resurrection. Knowing this, that our old man is crucified with him, that the body of sin might be destroyed, that henceforth we should not serve sin"* Romans 6:5-6.

Live for God-given dreams which are realized through the resurrection power within you – *"Work out your own salvation with fear and trembling. For it is God which worketh in you both to will and to do of his good pleasure"* Philippians 2:12, 13; 3:12.

Whether or not potential is developed depends on the invisible qualities we put into that potential: vision, faith, ingenuity, knowledge, talent and effort – Luke 9:12-17.

Self Test *Lesson 12*

1. To love someone is to work for his _____.

2. Being loving means being nice. _____ True _____ False

3. To feel deep remorse and regret is repentance. _____ True _____ False

4. Sorrow is a very strong negative that must be avoided at all costs. _____ True _____ False

5. Why does God chasten His children?

   _____

6. Conviction of sin is a sign of God's disappointment with us. _____ True _____ False

7. "Peace at any price" is a bad philosophy. _____ True _____ False

8. What is one supreme goal in every person's life? _____

9. What are some hindrances that prevent intimacy from developing?

   a. _____

   b. _____

   c. _____

10. If we will lose our life in Christ, we will _____.

11. Is it more important to learn to submit or to learn to resist? _____

12. What is God's transcendent glory, and what good does it do for you?

    _____

    _____

    _____

    _____

Keep this test for your own records.

Final Exam

1. _____ are the substance of every great achievement.

2. Use the following words to fill in the blanks below:

   personality   truth   principle   reality   pattern   character

   a. _____ and _____ are synonymous.

   b. Everything God does, He does according to a _____, based on a _____ of His Kingdom.

   c. The more we base our lives upon _____ and less upon _____, the straighter our course will be.

3. God will obligate Himself to help you achieve any dream.   ____ True   ____ False

4. All testing is based upon: *(circle one)*

   a. multiple choice   b. resistance   c. unhappiness

5. Perseverance will always outlast _____.

6. Use the following words to fill in the blanks below:

   philosophies   intimidated   tendency   failures   accept   rationalizations

   Men, whether ministers or laymen, have a _____ to be _____ by other

   men's _____ that are nothing more than _____ to justify

   failures. When you _____ such _____, you accept the _____ upon

   which they are based.

7. Poverty is a Godly, biblical principle that all God's people must embrace.   ____ True   ____ False

Final Exam

8. You will always grow only as far as the level of your _____.

9. What are the two basic things we do in life?

   a. _____   b. _____

10. What is one of the hardest things for men to do (a first step toward maturity)?

    _____

11. What is the "process" of life? _____

12. What is the "basis" of life? _____

13. The definition of both faith and fear is believing that something you cannot see will come to pass.

    ____ True   ____ False

    a. Faith attracts the _____.   b. Fear attracts the _____.

14. God ends everything on a _____.

15. From what come the characteristics of a kingdom? _____

16. What is the pivotal point between ruin and reconciliation? *(circle one)*

    a. rebellion   b. repentance   c. restoration

17. What type of men does God commit to? *(circle one)*

    a. able men   b. wise men   c. faithful men   d. talented men

18. What is one of life's greatest teachers? _____

19. God never gives authority without _____.

DETACH HERE

20. The real value of anything is always: *(circle one)*

    a. internal   b. external   c. fraternal

21. One of the most powerful things you can do in life is create: *(circle one)*

    a. a ministry   b. a newsletter   c. an image

22. Our willingness to _____ qualifies us to lead others.

23. The measure of our greatness is seen in how we _____ for others.

24. Every leader is limited by three things in his life. What are they?

    a. _____

    b. _____

    c. _____

25. What must happen before we, as men or ministers, can publicly denounce sin?

    _____

26. Preach the _____; practice your _____.

27. The place of agreement is the place of _____.

28. A kingdom principle is that you are committed to what you confess.   ____ True   ____ False

29. We confess _____ sin, and confess _____ righteousness.

30. Match the following:

    ____ Repentance must be balanced by   a. the key to life

    ____ Believing must be balanced by   b. toughness

    ____ Tenderness must be balanced by   c. receiving

    ____ Balance is   d. faith

31. Life is composed of your _____ and constructed by your _____.

32. God wants us to speak out or confess our dreams. ____ True ____ False

33. What is the criteria for holiness? _____

34. Decision always translates into _____.

35. When you conquer temptation one time, it will never bother you again. ____ True ____ False

36. It doesn't matter what you believe about God because He's going to do what He wants anyway.

    ____ True ____ False

37. What you believe about God holds the greatest potential for good or harm in life.

    ____ True ____ False

38. When God convicts us of sin, it is an expression of His anger toward us.

    ____ True ____ False

39. By not forgiving your parents, you can actually retain their sins in your life.

    ____ True ____ False

40. Pressure always _____.

Final Exam

41. The difference between men who succeed or men who fail is their ability to handle _____.

42. Some things in life are: _____

43. The use of money is a visible expression of _____.

44. Name the three areas of your life from which you should be tithing

    a. _____   b. _____   c. _____

45. Which is correct? *(check one)*

    ____ Money is the root of all evil.

    ____ The love of money is the root of all evil.

46. Obedience is the evidence of _____.

47. We cannot _____ by sacrifice what we lose through _____.

48. What is the cure for guilt? *(circle one)*

    a. prayer   b. fasting   c. forgiveness

49. Once God has forgiven you, you must forgive _____.

50. The way you'll know that you really forgave is that you completely forget.   ____ True   ____ False

51. Holding on to a little guilt can be a good thing, as it will keep us humble.   ____ True   ____ False

52. If we do not forgive ourselves of our sins, what have we done in relationship to God?

    _____

53. To love someone is to work for his _____.

54. "Peace at any price" is a bad philosophy.   ____ True   ____ False

55. If we will lose our life in Christ, we will _____.

Final Exam

56. Short Essay: "Everything in life holds potential." Analyze that statement, giving examples of real life situations where it has proven to be true. Summarize how that statement holds true in your daily life, giving an example of how you have recently applied it. (Did potential for good or evil turn out for the good because of the way you approached it?)

_____

_____

_____

_____

_____

_____

_____

_____

_____

Name _____

Address _____ City _____ State____ Zip_____

Telephone a.m. _____ p.m. _____

Email Address _____

The Final Exam is required to be "commissioned."

For more information, contact
Christian Men's Network | P.O. Box 3 | Grapevine, TX 76099
ChristianMensNetwork.com | office@ChristianMensNetwork.com | 817-437-4888

DETACH HERE

Basic Daily Bible Reading

Read Proverbs each morning for wisdom, Psalms each evening for courage. Make copies of this chart and keep it in your Bible to mark off as you read. If you are just starting the habit of Bible reading, be aware that longer translations or paraphrases (such as Amplified and Living) will take longer to read each day. As you start, it is okay to read only one of the chapters in Psalms each night, instead of the many listed. Mark your chart so you'll remember which ones you haven't read.

NOTE: The chronological chart following has the rest of the chapters of Psalms that are not listed here. By using both charts together, you will cover the entire book of Psalms.

Day of Month	Proverbs	Psalms	Day of Month	Proverbs	Psalms
1	1	1, 2, 4, 5, 6	18	18	82, 83, 84, 85
2	2	7, 8, 9	19	19	87, 88, 91, 92
3	3	10, 11, 12, 13, 14, 15	20	20	93, 94, 95, 97
4	4	16, 17, 19, 20	21	21	98, 99, 100, 101, 103
5	5	21, 22, 23	22	22	104, 108
6	6	24, 25, 26, 27	23	23	109, 110, 111
7	7	28, 29, 31, 32	24	24	112, 113, 114, 115, 117
8	8	33, 35	25	25	119:1-56
9	9	36, 37	26	26	119:57-112
10	10	38, 39, 40	27	27	119:113-176
11	11	41, 42, 43, 45, 46	28	28	120, 121, 122, 124, 130, 131, 133, 134
12	12	47, 48, 49, 50			
13	13	53, 55, 58, 61, 62	29	29	135, 136, 138
14	14	64, 65, 66, 67	30	30	139, 140, 141, 143
15	15	68, 69	31	31	144, 145, 146, 148, 150
16	16	70, 71, 73			
17	17	75, 76, 77, 81			

Chronological Annual Bible Reading

This schedule follows the events of the Bible chronologically and can be used with any translation or paraphrase of the Bible. Each day has an average of 77 verses of Scripture. If you follow this annually, along with your Daily Bible Reading, by your third year, you will recognize where you are and what is going to happen next. By your fifth year, you will understand the Scriptural background and setting for any reference spoken of in a message or book. At that point, the Word will become more like "meat" to you and less like "milk." Once you understand the basic stories and what happens on the surface, God can reveal to you the layers of meaning beneath. So, make copies of this chart to keep in your Bible and mark off as you read. And start reading—it's the greatest adventure in life!

Some notes:

1. Some modern translations don't have verses numbered (such as The Message), so they cannot be used with this chart. Also, if you are just starting the Bible, be aware that longer translations or paraphrases (such as Amplified and Living) tend to take longer to read each day.

2. The Daily Bible Reading chart covers the Proverbs and the chapters of Psalms that are not listed here. By using both charts together, you will cover the entire books of Psalms and Proverbs along with the rest of the Bible.

3. The chronology of Scripture is obvious in some cases, educated guesswork in others. The placement of Job, for example, is purely conjecture since there is no consensus among Bible scholars as to its date or place. For the most part, however, chronological reading helps the reader, since it places stories that have duplicated information, or prophetic utterances elsewhere in Scripture, within the same reading sequence.

HOW TO READ SCRIPTURE NOTATIONS:

Book chapter: verse. (Mark 15:44 means the book of Mark, chapter 15, verse 44.)

Book chapter; chapter (Mark 15; 16; 17 means the book of Mark, chapters 15, 16, 17.)

Books continue the same until otherwise noted. (2 Kings 22; 23:1-28; Jeremiah 20 means the book of 2 Kings, chapter 22, the book of 2 Kings, chapter 23, verses 1-28; then the book of Jeremiah, chapter 20.)

DETACH HERE

#	Date	Reading
1	Jan 1	Genesis 1; 2; 3
2	Jan 2	Genesis 4; 5; 6
3	Jan 3	Genesis 7; 8; 9
4	Jan 4	Genesis 10; 11; 12
5	Jan 5	Genesis 13; 14; 15; 16
6	Jan 6	Genesis 17; 18; 19:1-29
7	Jan 7	Genesis 19:30-38; 20; 21
8	Jan 8	Genesis 22; 23; 24:1-31
9	Jan 9	Genesis 24:32-67; 25
10	Jan 10	Genesis 26; 27
11	Jan 11	Genesis 28; 29; 30:1-24
12	Jan 12	Genesis 30:25-43; 31
13	Jan 13	Genesis 32; 33; 34
14	Jan 14	Genesis 35; 36
15	Jan 15	Genesis 37; 38; 39
16	Jan 16	Genesis 40; 41
17	Jan 17	Genesis 42; 43
18	Jan 18	Genesis 44; 45
19	Jan 19	Genesis 46; 47; 48
20	Jan 20	Genesis 49; 50; Exodus 1
21	Jan 21	Exodus 2; 3; 4
22	Jan 22	Exodus 5; 6; 7
23	Jan 23	Exodus 8; 9
24	Jan 24	Exodus 10; 11; 12
25	Jan 25	Exodus 13; 14; 15
26	Jan 26	Exodus 16; 17; 18
27	Jan 27	Exodus 19; 20; 21
28	Jan 28	Exodus 22; 23; 24
29	Jan 29	Exodus 25; 26
30	Jan 30	Exodus 27; 28; 29:1-28
31	Jan 31	Exodus 29:29-46; 30; 31
32	Feb 1	Exodus 32; 33; 34
33	Feb 2	Exodus 35; 36
34	Feb 3	Exodus 37; 38
35	Feb 4	Exodus 39; 40
36	Feb 5	Leviticus 1; 2; 3; 4
37	Feb 6	Leviticus 5; 6; 7
38	Feb 7	Leviticus 8; 9; 10
39	Feb 8	Leviticus 11; 12; 13:1-37
40	Feb 9	Leviticus 13:38-59; 14
41	Feb 10	Leviticus 15; 16
42	Feb 11	Leviticus 17; 18; 19
43	Feb 12	Leviticus 20; 21; 22:1-16
44	Feb 13	Leviticus 22:17-33; 23
45	Feb 14	Leviticus 24; 25
46	Feb 15	Leviticus 26; 27
47	Feb 16	Numbers 1; 2
48	Feb 17	Numbers 3; 4:1-20
49	Feb 18	Numbers 4:21-49; 5; 6
50	Feb 19	Numbers 7
51	Feb 20	Numbers 8; 9; 10
52	Feb 21	Numbers 11; 12; 13
53	Feb 22	Numbers 14; 15
54	Feb 23	Numbers 16; 17
55	Feb 24	Numbers 18; 19; 20
56	Feb 25	Numbers 21; 22
57	Feb 26	Numbers 23; 24; 25
58	Feb 27	Numbers 26; 27
59	Feb 28	Numbers 28; 29; 30
60	Mar 1	Numbers 31; 32:1-27
61	Mar 2	Numbers 32:28-42; 33
62	Mar 3	Numbers 34; 35; 36
63	Mar 4	Deuteronomy 1; 2
64	Mar 5	Deuteronomy 3; 4
65	Mar 6	Deuteronomy 5; 6; 7
66	Mar 7	Deuteronomy 8; 9; 10
67	Mar 8	Deuteronomy 11; 12; 13
68	Mar 9	Deuteronomy 14; 15; 16
69	Mar 10	Deuteronomy 17; 18; 19; 20
70	Mar 11	Deuteronomy 21; 22; 23
71	Mar 12	Deuteronomy 24; 25; 26; 27
72	Mar 13	Deuteronomy 28
73	Mar 14	Deuteronomy 29; 30; 31
74	Mar 15	Deuteronomy 32; 33
75	Mar 16	Deuteronomy 34; Psalm 90; Joshua 1; 2
76	Mar 17	Joshua 3; 4; 5; 6
77	Mar 18	Joshua 7; 8; 9
78	Mar 19	Joshua 10; 11
79	Mar 20	Joshua 12; 13; 14
80	Mar 21	Joshua 15; 16
81	Mar 22	Joshua 17; 18; 19:1-23
82	Mar 23	Joshua 19:24-51; 20; 21
83	Mar 24	Joshua 22; 23; 24
84	Mar 25	Judges 1; 2; 3:1-11
85	Mar 26	Judges 3:12-31; 4; 5
86	Mar 27	Judges 6; 7
87	Mar 28	Judges 8; 9
88	Mar 29	Judges 10; 11; 12
89	Mar 30	Judges 13; 14; 15
90	Mar 31	Judges 16; 17; 18
91	Apr 1	Judges 19; 20
		[You have completed 1/4 of the Bible!]
92	Apr 2	Judges 21; Job 1; 2; 3
93	Apr 3	Job 4; 5; 6
94	Apr 4	Job 7; 8; 9
95	Apr 5	Job 10; 11; 12
96	Apr 6	Job 13; 14; 15
97	Apr 7	Job 16; 17; 18; 19
98	Apr 8	Job 20; 21
99	Apr 9	Job 22; 23; 24
100	Apr 10	Job 25; 26; 27; 28
101	Apr 11	Job 29; 30; 31
102	Apr 12	Job 32; 33; 34
103	Apr 13	Job 35; 36; 37
104	Apr 14	Job 38; 39
105	Apr 15	Job 40; 41; 42
106	Apr 16	Ruth 1; 2; 3
107	Apr 17	Ruth 4; 1 Samuel 1; 2
108	Apr 18	1 Samuel 3; 4; 5; 6
109	Apr 19	1 Samuel 7; 8; 9
110	Apr 20	1 Samuel 10; 11; 12; 13
111	Apr 21	1 Samuel 14; 15
112	Apr 22	1 Samuel 16; 17
113	Apr 23	1 Samuel 18; 19; Psalm 59
114	Apr 24	1 Samuel 20; 21; Psalms 34; 56
115	Apr 25	1 Samuel 22; 23; Psalms 52; 142
116	Apr 26	1 Samuel 24; 25; 1 Chronicles 12:8-18; Psalm 57
117	Apr 27	1 Samuel 26; 27; 28; Psalms 54; 63
118	Apr 28	1 Samuel 29; 30; 31; 1 Chronicles 12:1-7; 12:19-22
119	Apr 29	1 Chronicles 10; 2 Samuel 1; 2
120	Apr 30	2 Samuel 3; 4; 1 Chronicles 11:1-9; 12:23-40
121	May 1	2 Samuel 5; 6; 1 Chronicles 13; 14
122	May 2	2 Samuel 22; 1 Chronicles 15
123	May 3	1 Chronicles 16; Psalm 18
124	May 4	2 Samuel 7; Psalms 96; 105
125	May 5	1 Chronicles 17; 2 Samuel 8; 9; 10
126	May 6	1 Chronicles 18; 19; Psalm 60; 2 Samuel 11
127	May 7	2 Samuel 12; 13; 1 Chronicles 20:1-3; Psalm 51
128	May 8	2 Samuel 14; 15
129	May 9	2 Samuel 16; 17; 18; Psalm 3
130	May 10	2 Samuel 19; 20; 21
131	May 11	2 Samuel 23:8-23
132	May 12	1 Chronicles 20:4-8; 11:10-25; 2 Samuel 23:24-39; 24
133	May 13	1 Chronicles 11:26-47; 21; 22
134	May 14	1 Chronicles 23; 24; Psalm 30
135	May 15	1 Chronicles 25; 26
136	May 16	1 Chronicles 27; 28; 29
137	May 17	1 Kings 1; 2:1-12; 2 Samuel 23:1-7
138	May 18	1 Kings 2:13-46; 3; 2 Chronicles 1:1-13
139	May 19	1 Kings 5; 6; 2 Chronicles 2
140	May 20	1 Kings 7; 2 Chronicles 3; 4
141	May 21	1 Kings 8; 2 Chronicles 5
142	May 22	1 Kings 9; 2 Chronicles 6; 7:1-10
143	May 23	1 Kings 10:1-13; 2 Chronicles 7:11-22; 8; 9:1-12; 1 Kings 4
144	May 24	1 Kings 10:14-29; 2 Chronicles 1:14-17; 9:13-28; Psalms 72; 127
145	May 25	Song of Solomon 1; 2; 3; 4; 5
146	May 26	Song of Solomon 6; 7; 8; 1 Kings 11:1-40
147	May 27	Ecclesiastes 1; 2; 3; 4
148	May 28	Ecclesiastes 5; 6; 7; 8
149	May 29	Ecclesiastes 9; 10; 11; 12; 1 Kings 11:41-43; 2 Chronicles 9:29-31
150	May 30	1 Kings 12; 2 Chronicles 10; 11
151	May 31	1 Kings 13; 14; 2 Chronicles 12
152	June 1	1 Kings 15; 2 Chronicles 13; 14; 15
153	June 2	1 Kings 16; 2 Chronicles 16; 17
154	June 3	1 Kings 17; 18; 19
155	June 4	1 Kings 20; 21
156	June 5	1 Kings 22; 2 Chronicles 18
157	June 6	2 Kings 1; 2; 2 Chronicles 19; 20; 21:1-3
158	June 7	2 Kings 3; 4
159	June 8	2 Kings 5; 6; 7
160	June 9	2 Kings 8; 9; 2 Chronicles 21:4-20
161	June 10	2 Chronicles 22; 23; 2 Kings 10; 11
162	June 11	Joel 1; 2; 3
163	June 12	2 Kings 12; 13; 2 Chronicles 24
164	June 13	2 Kings 14; 2 Chronicles 25; Jonah 1

165	June 14	Jonah 2; 3; 4; Hosea 1; 2; 3; 4
166	June 15	Hosea 5; 6; 7; 8; 9; 10
167	June 16	Hosea 11; 12; 13; 14
168	June 17	2 Kings 15:1-7;
		2 Chronicles 26; Amos 1; 2; 3
169	June 18	Amos 4; 5; 6; 7
170	June 19	Amos 8; 9; 2 Kings 15:8-18;
		Isaiah 1
171	June 20	Isaiah 2; 3; 4; 2 Kings 15:19-38;
		2 Chronicles 27
172	June 21	Isaiah 5; 6; Micah 1; 2; 3
173	June 22	Micah 4; 5; 6; 7; 2 Kings 16:1-18
174	June 23	2 Chronicles 28; Isaiah 7; 8
175	June 24	Isaiah 9; 10; 11; 12
176	June 25	Isaiah 13; 14; 15; 16
177	June 26	Isaiah 17; 18; 19; 20; 21
178	June 27	Isaiah 22; 23; 24; 25
179	June 28	Isaiah 26; 27; 28; 29
180	June 29	Isaiah 30; 31; 32; 33
181	June 30	Isaiah 34; 35; 2 Kings 18:1-8;
		2 Chronicles 29
182	July 1	2 Chronicles 30; 31; 2 Kings 17;
		2 Kings 16:19-20
		[You have completed 1/2 of the Bible!]
183	July 2	2 Kings 18:9-37;
		2 Chronicles 32:1-19; Isaiah 36
184	July 3	2 Kings 19; 2 Chronicles 32:20-23;
		Isaiah 37
185	July 4	2 Kings 20; 21:1-18; 2 Chronicles
		32:24-33; Isaiah 38; 39
186	July 5	2 Chronicles 33:1-20; Isaiah 40; 41
187	July 6	Isaiah 42; 43; 44
188	July 7	Isaiah 45; 46; 47; 48
189	July 8	Isaiah 49; 50; 51; 52
190	July 9	Isaiah 53; 54; 55; 56; 57
191	July 10	Isaiah 58; 59; 60; 61; 62
192	July 11	Isaiah 63; 64; 65; 66
193	July 12	2 Kings 21:19-26; 2 Chronicles
		33:21-25; 34:1-7; Zephaniah 1; 2; 3
194	July 13	Jeremiah 1; 2; 3
195	July 14	Jeremiah 4; 5
196	July 15	Jeremiah 6; 7; 8
197	July 16	Jeremiah 9; 10; 11
198	July 17	Jeremiah 12; 13; 14; 15
199	July 18	Jeremiah 16; 17; 18; 19
200	July 19	Jeremiah 20; 2 Kings 22; 23:1-28
201	July 20	2 Chronicles 34:8-33; 35:1-19;
		Nahum 1; 2; 3
202	July 21	2 Kings 23:29-37; 2 Chronicles
		35:20-27; 36:1-5; Jeremiah
		22:10-17; 26; Habakkuk 1
203	July 22	Habakkuk 2; 3; Jeremiah 46; 47;
		2 Kings 24:1-4; 2 Chronicles 36:6-7
204	July 23	Jeremiah 25; 35; 36; 45
205	July 24	Jeremiah 48; 49:1-33
206	July 25	Daniel 1; 2
207	July 26	Jeremiah 22:18-30; 2 Kings
		24:5-20; 2 Chronicles 36:8-12;
		Jeremiah 37:1-2; 52:1-3; 24; 29

208	July 27	Jeremiah 27; 28; 23
209	July 28	Jeremiah 50; 51:1-19
210	July 29	Jeremiah 51:20-64; 49:34-39; 34
211	July 30	Ezekiel 1; 2; 3; 4
212	July 31	Ezekiel 5; 6; 7; 8
213	Aug 1	Ezekiel 9; 10; 11; 12
214	Aug 2	Ezekiel 13, 14, 15, 16:1-34
215	Aug 3	Ezekiel 16:35-63; 17; 18
216	Aug 4	Ezekiel 19; 20
217	Aug 5	Ezekiel 21; 22
218	Aug 6	Ezekiel 23; 2 Kings 25:1;
		2 Chronicles 36:13-16;
		Jeremiah 39:1; 52:4; Ezekiel 24
219	Aug 7	Jeremiah 21; 22:1-9; 32; 30
220	Aug 8	Jeremiah 31; 33; Ezekiel 25
221	Aug 9	Ezekiel 29:1-16; 30; 31; 26
222	Aug 10	Ezekiel 27; 28; Jeremiah 37:3-21
223	Aug 11	Jeremiah 38; 39:2-10; 52:5-30
224	Aug 12	2 Kings 25:2-22; 2 Chronicles
		36:17-21; Jeremiah 39:11-18;
		40:1-6; Lamentations 1
225	Aug 13	Lamentations 2; 3
226	Aug 14	Lamentations 4; 5; Obadiah;
		Jeremiah 40:7-16
227	Aug 15	Jeremiah 41; 42; 43; 44;
		2 Kings 25:23-26
228	Aug 16	Ezekiel 33:21-33; 34; 35; 36
229	Aug 17	Ezekiel 37; 38; 39
230	Aug 18	Ezekiel 32; 33:1-20; Daniel 3
231	Aug 19	Ezekiel 40; 41
232	Aug 20	Ezekiel 42; 43; 44
233	Aug 21	Ezekiel 45; 46; 47
234	Aug 22	Ezekiel 48; 29:17-21; Daniel 4
235	Aug 23	Jeremiah 52:31-34; 2 Kings
		25:27-30; Psalms 44; 74; 79
236	Aug 24	Psalms 80; 86; 89
237	Aug 25	Psalms 102; 106
238	Aug 26	Psalms 123; 137; Daniel 7; 8
239	Aug 27	Daniel 5; 9; 6
240	Aug 28	2 Chronicles 36:22-23; Ezra 1; 2
241	Aug 29	Ezra 3; 4:1-5; Daniel 10; 11
242	Aug 30	Daniel 12; Ezra 4:6-24; 5;
		6:1-13; Haggai 1
243	Aug 31	Haggai 2; Zechariah 1; 2; 3
244	Sept 1	Zechariah 4; 5; 6; 7; 8
245	Sept 2	Ezra 6:14-22; Psalm 78
246	Sept 3	Psalms 107; 116; 118
247	Sept 4	Psalms 125; 126; 128; 129;
		132; 147
248	Sept 5	Psalm 149; Zechariah 9; 10;
		11; 12; 13
249	Sept 6	Zechariah 14; Esther 1; 2; 3
250	Sept 7	Esther 4; 5; 6; 7; 8
251	Sept 8	Esther 9; 10; Ezra 7; 8
252	Sept 9	Ezra 9; 10; Nehemiah 1
253	Sept 10	Nehemiah 2; 3; 4; 5
254	Sept 11	Nehemiah 6; 7
255	Sept 12	Nehemiah 8; 9; 10
256	Sept 13	Nehemiah 11; 12
257	Sept 14	Nehemiah 13; Malachi 1; 2; 3; 4

258	Sept 15	1 Chronicles 1; 2:1-35
259	Sept 16	1 Chronicles 2:36-55; 3; 4
260	Sept 17	1 Chronicles 5; 6:1-41
261	Sept 18	1 Chronicles 6:42-81; 7
262	Sept 19	1 Chronicles 8; 9
263	Sept 20	Matthew 1; 2; 3; 4
264	Sept 21	Matthew 5; 6
265	Sept 22	Matthew 7; 8
266	Sept 23	Matthew 9; 10
267	Sept 24	Matthew 11; 12
268	Sept 25	Matthew 13; 14
269	Sept 26	Matthew 15; 16
270	Sept 27	Matthew 17; 18; 19
271	Sept 28	Matthew 20; 21
272	Sept 29	Matthew 22; 23
273	Sept 30	Matthew 24; 25
		[You have completed 3/4 of the Bible!]
274	Oct 1	Matthew 26; 27; 28
275	Oct 2	Mark 1; 2
276	Oct 3	Mark 3; 4
277	Oct 4	Mark 5; 6
278	Oct 5	Mark 7; 8:1-26
279	Oct 6	Mark 8:27-38; 9
280	Oct 7	Mark 10; 11
281	Oct 8	Mark 12; 13
282	Oct 9	Mark 14
283	Oct 10	Mark 15; 16
284	Oct 11	Luke 1
285	Oct 12	Luke 2; 3
286	Oct 13	Luke 4; 5
287	Oct 14	Luke 6; 7:1-23
288	Oct 15	Luke 7:24-50; 8
289	Oct 16	Luke 9
290	Oct 17	Luke 10; 11
291	Oct 18	Luke 12; 13
292	Oct 19	Luke 14; 15
293	Oct 20	Luke 16; 17
294	Oct 21	Luke 18; 19
295	Oct 22	Luke 20; 21
296	Oct 23	Luke 22
297	Oct 24	Luke 23; 24:1-28
298	Oct 25	Luke 24:29-53; John 1
299	Oct 26	John 2; 3; 4:1-23
300	Oct 27	John 4:24-54; 5; 6:1-7
301	Oct 28	John 6:8-71; 7:1-21
302	Oct 29	John 7:22-53; 8
303	Oct 30	John 9; 10
304	Oct 31	John 11; 12:1-28
305	Nov 1	John 12:29-50; 13; 14
306	Nov 2	John 15; 16; 17
307	Nov 3	John 18; 19:1-24
308	Nov 4	John 19:25-42; 20; 21
309	Nov 5	Acts 1; 2
310	Nov 6	Acts 3; 4
311	Nov 7	Acts 5; 6
312	Nov 8	Acts 7
313	Nov 9	Acts 8; 9
314	Nov 10	Acts 10
315	Nov 11	Acts 11
316	Nov 12	Acts 12; 13

317	Nov 13	Acts 14; 15; Galatians 1
318	Nov 14	Galatians 2; 3; 4
319	Nov 15	Galatians 5; 6; James 1
320	Nov 16	James 2; 3; 4; 5
321	Nov 17	Acts 16; 17
322	Nov 18	Acts 18:1-11; 1 Thessalonians 1; 2; 3; 4
323	Nov 19	1 Thessalonians 5; 2 Thessalonians 1; 2; 3
324	Nov 20	Acts 18:12-28; 19:1-22; 1 Corinthians 1
325	Nov 21	1 Corinthians 2; 3; 4; 5
326	Nov 22	1 Corinthians 6; 7; 8
327	Nov 23	1 Corinthians 9; 10; 11
328	Nov 24	1 Corinthians 12; 13; 14
329	Nov 25	1 Corinthians 15; 16
330	Nov 26	Acts 19:23-41; 20:1; 2 Corinthians 1; 2
331	Nov 27	2 Corinthians 3; 4; 5
332	Nov 28	2 Corinthians 6; 7; 8; 9
333	Nov 29	2 Corinthians 10; 11; 12
334	Nov 30	2 Corinthians 13; Romans 1; 2
335	Dec 1	Romans 3; 4; 5
336	Dec 2	Romans 6; 7; 8
337	Dec 3	Romans 9; 10; 11
338	Dec 4	Romans 12; 13; 14
339	Dec 5	Romans 15; 16
340	Dec 6	Acts 20:2-38; 21
341	Dec 7	Acts 22; 23
342	Dec 8	Acts 24; 25; 26
343	Dec 9	Acts 27; 28
344	Dec 10	Ephesians 1; 2; 3
345	Dec 11	Ephesians 4; 5; 6
346	Dec 12	Colossians 1; 2; 3
347	Dec 13	Colossians 4; Philippians 1; 2
348	Dec 14	Philippians 3; 4; Philemon
349	Dec 15	1 Timothy 1; 2; 3; 4
350	Dec 16	1 Timothy 5; 6; Titus 1; 2
351	Dec 17	Titus 3; 2 Timothy 1; 2; 3
352	Dec 18	2 Timothy 4; 1 Peter 1; 2
353	Dec 19	1 Peter 3; 4; 5; Jude
354	Dec 20	2 Peter 1; 2; 3; Hebrews 1
355	Dec 21	Hebrews 2; 3; 4; 5
356	Dec 22	Hebrews 6; 7; 8; 9
357	Dec 23	Hebrews 10; 11
358	Dec 24	Hebrews 12; 13; 2 John; 3 John
359	Dec 25	1 John 1; 2; 3; 4
360	Dec 26	1 John 5; Revelation 1; 2
361	Dec 27	Revelation 3; 4; 5; 6
362	Dec 28	Revelation 7; 8; 9; 10; 11
363	Dec 29	Revelation 12; 13; 14; 15
364	Dec 30	Revelation 16; 17; 18; 19
365	Dec 31	Revelation 20; 21; 22

You have completed the entire Bible-Congratulations!

MANHOOD GROWTH PLAN

Order the corresponding workbook for each book, and study the first four Majoring In Men® Curriculum books in this order:

MAXIMIZED MANHOOD: Realize your need for God in every area of your life and start mending relationships with Christ and your family.

COURAGE: Make peace with your past, learn the power of forgiveness and the value of character. Let yourself be challenged to speak up for Christ to other men.

COMMUNICATION, SEX AND MONEY: Increase your ability to communicate, place the right values on sex and money in relationships, and greatly improve relationships, whether married or single.

STRONG MEN IN TOUGH TIMES: Reframe trials, battles and discouragement in light of Scripture and gain solid footing for business, career, and relational choices in the future.

Choose five of the following books to study next. When you have completed nine books, if you are not in men's group, you can find a Majoring In Men® group near you and become "commissioned" to minister to other men.

DARING: Overcome fear to live a life of daring ambition for Godly pursuits.

SEXUAL INTEGRITY: Recognize the sacredness of the sexual union, overcome mistakes and blunders and commit to righteousness in your sexuality.

UNIQUE WOMAN: Discover what makes a woman tick, from adolescence through maturity, to be able to minister to a spouse's uniqueness at any age.

NEVER QUIT: Take the ten steps for entering or leaving any situation, job, relationship or crisis in life.

REAL MAN: Discover the deepest meaning of Christlikeness and learn to exercise good character in times of stress, success or failure.

POWER OF POTENTIAL: Start making solid business and career choices based on Biblical principles while building core character that affects your entire life.

ABSOLUTE ANSWERS: Adopt practical habits and pursue Biblical solutions to overcome "prodigal problems" and secret sins that hinder both success and satisfaction with life.

TREASURE: Practice Biblical solutions and principles on the job to find treasures such as the satisfaction of exercising integrity and a job well done.

IRRESISTIBLE HUSBAND: Avoid common mistakes that sabotage a relationship and learn simple solutions and good habits to build a marriage that will consistently increase in intensity for decades.

MAJORING IN MEN® CURRICULUM

CHURCH GROWTH PLAN
STRONG - SUSTAINABLE - SYNERGISTIC

THREE PRACTICAL PHASES TO A POWERFUL MEN'S MOVEMENT IN YOUR CHURCH

Phase One:

- Pastor disciples key men/men's director using Maximized Manhood system.

- Launch creates momentum among men

- Church becomes more attractive to hold men who visit

- Families grow stronger

- Men increase bond to pastor

Phase Two:

- Men/men's director teach other men within the church

- Increased tithing and giving by men

- Decreased number of families in crisis

- Increased mentoring of teens and children

- Increase of male volunteers

- Faster assimilation for men visitors - clear path for pastor to connect with new men

- Men pray regularly for pastor

Phase Three:

- Men teach other men outside the church and bring them to Christ

- Increased male population and attraction to a visiting man, seeing a place he belongs

- Stronger, better-attended community outreaches

- Men are loyal to and support pastor

This system enables the pastor to successfully train key leaders, create momentum, build a church that attracts and holds men who visit, and disciple strong men.

Churches may conduct men's ministry entirely free of charge!
Learn how by calling 817-437-4888.

CONTACT
MAJORING IN MEN® CURRICULUM
817-437-4888
admin@ChristianMensNetwork.com

Christian Men's Network
P.O. Box 3
Grapevine, TX 76099

Great discounts available.

Start your discipleship TODAY!

Call today for group discounts
and coaching opportunities.

FREE DVD!
Send your name and address to:
office@ChristianMensNetwork.com
We'll send you a FREE full-length DVD
with ministry for men.
(Limit one per person.)

ABOUT THE AUTHOR

Edwin Louis Cole mentored hundreds of thousands of people through challenging events and powerful books that have become the most widely-used Christian men's resources in the world. He is known for pithy statements and a confrontational style that demanded social responsibility and family leadership.

After serving as a pastor, evangelist, and Christian television pioneer, and at an age when most men were retiring, he followed his greatest passion—to lead men into Christlikeness, which he called "real manhood."

Ed Cole was a real man through and through. A loving son to earthly parents and the heavenly Father. Devoted husband to the "loveliest lady in the land," Nancy Corbett Cole. Dedicated father to three and, over the years, accepting the role of "father" to thousands. A reader, a thinker, a visionary. A man who made mistakes, learned lessons, then shared the wealth of his wisdom with men around the world. The Christian Men's Network he founded in 1977 is still a vibrant, global ministry. Unquestionably, he was the greatest men's minister of his generation.

Facebook.com/EdwinLouisCole